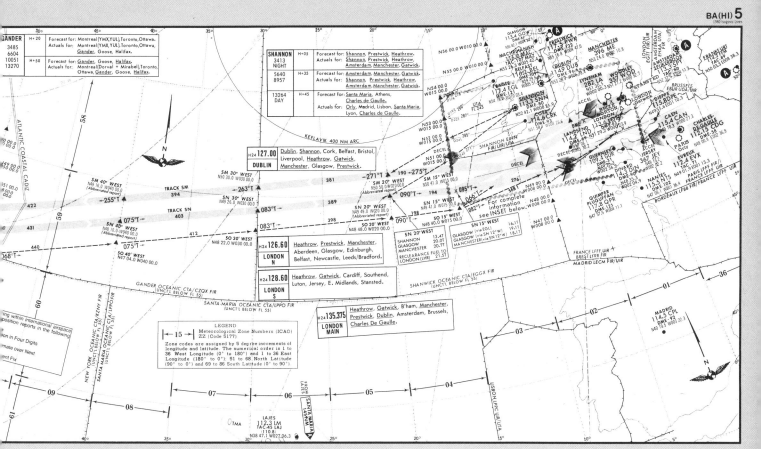

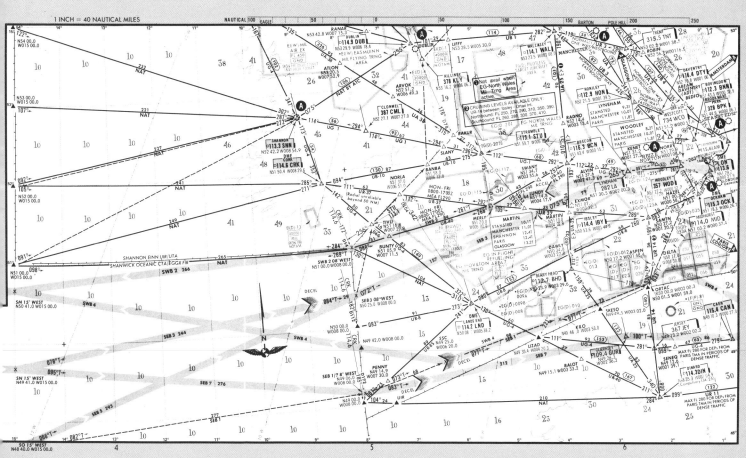

THE
CONCORDE
STORY

THE
CONCORDE
STORY

Ten Years in Service

Christopher Orlebar

TEMPLE PRESS

Endpapers

These charts show Concorde's west
and east bound Atlantic tracks,
'SM' and 'SN' respectively; 'SO' is a
reserve track. The acceleration and
deceleration points, labelled
'ACCEL' and 'DECEL', are the
points respectively where
Concorde either commences
acceleration from Mach 0.95, or
deceleration from Mach 2. However,
the deceleration point is varied a
few miles either side of the position
shown depending on the conditions
– aircraft altitude and forecast wind
– prevalent on the day.

    There are a variety of routes into
the United States, however the
route to New York via Linnd and
Sates is the one described in the
chapter, The Flight – Deceleration.
Concorde must cross the boundary
of the 'warning area' (W105 BDY)
above 52,000 ft when that area is
'active' with military training or
test flights.

    The front inset shows a plan view
of the runways at Heathrow. The
back inset shows the approach path
to runway 4R at Kennedy – the
runway onto which the landing was
made in the chapter, The Flight –
Deceleration.

Half title page

One of the few photographs taken
of Concorde actually in supersonic
flight. This picture was taken from
a Panavia Tornado.

To my wife Nicola and our children Edward and Caroline. CO

Published by Temple Press
an imprint of The Hamlyn Publishing Group Limited,
Bridge House, 69 London Road, Twickenham, Middlesex, TW1 3SB
and distributed for them by
Hamlyn Distribution Services
Rushden, Northants, England

© Newnes Books 1986

First published 1986
Fifth impression 1987

ISBN 0 600 33369 8

Printed in Italy

Contents

Acknowledgements

Contemplation of this book was simple, but without the cooperation and encouragement of a great many people writing it, as a practising pilot earning my bread and butter with British Airways, would have been a daunting prospect. In particular, I would like to thank Brian Walpole for his suggesting that I should be its author – it was his idea that this book should appear on the tenth anniversary of Concorde's commercial operations. I would also like to thank Mike Ramsden editor-in-chief of *Flight International* who reinforced that confidence. Especially I would like to thank my children, Edward and Caroline for putting up with me closetted for hours in my study during their summer holidays; my wife, Nicola, and my sister-in-law, Angela Metcalf, who deciphered my writing and turned it into a typewritten manuscript. My neighbours, Peter Leggett, Fellow of the Royal Aeronautical Society and former Vice-Chancellor of Surrey University, and his wife, Enid, have given immense assistance, reading and suggesting many improvements in the manuscript. Also, Charles Burnet of British Aerospace at Weybridge, whose book *Three Centuries to Concorde* reinforced my enthusiasm for the historical side of supersonic flight, has carefully checked my historical and technical facts, and my expressing of them.

The greatest acknowledgement must go to the people who designed, built, maintain and fly Concorde and to the passengers who ensured the ultimate success of Concorde. Without them this extraordinary aircraft would have come to nought and there would have been no story.

Christopher Orlebar
Oxshott, October 1985

The author with Sir Frank Whittle on the flight deck of Concorde during the filming of 'Jet Trail', a documentary about the effect of jet propulsion on civil transport. May 1984

Foreword

by Captain Brian Walpole

Concorde is an outstanding aeroplane, it is a technical miracle, and more. For the men who designed and constructed it, the crews who tested it, for those in British Airways involved in its operation – flying it, maintaining it, marketing it – and for its passengers, Concorde is a way of life.

The story of Concorde is a story of survival. In its long history, it has been vulnerable in four main areas. Technically, environmentally, politically and economically. Many times it has stood close to extinction. But it survived, thanks to the dedication, faith and belief of those who controlled its destiny at the various critical phases of its life.

Its design, construction and maintenance teams have overcome many and varied problems, and now, ten years into airline service, we have a safe, proven, reliable and totally unparalleled piece of aviation technology flying the world's air routes. It is confidently predicted that it will fly into the 21st century; many indeed suggest that this is where its technology came from in the first place.

Politically, it has come through the vicissitudes of national and international politics until, today, it stands free from political influence. Environmentally, its operation has been skilfully tailored to meet acceptance almost worldwide. Economically, it represents a major contribution to British Airways' profitability and a unique asset of unquantifiable value as the airline's flagship.

The faith of those who believed that Concorde represented a technical achievement of enormous magnitude which should not be allowed to perish, has been fully vindicated. All who have contributed to this magnificent aircraft and the way of life it represents are today justifiably proud of 'the beautiful bird – Concorde'.

Captain
Brian Walpole,
General Manager,
Concorde Division
of British Airways

H.M. The Queen Mother's birthday present from British Airways was a trip in Concorde on 6 August 1985. Seen here with Captain Walpole (centre) and Senior Engineer Officer, Peter Phillips (right)

Preface

This book is about the conquest of flight at speeds faster than sound. It covers the synthesis of the host of disciplines which were brought together to build and operate the most superlative form of transport yet built by man – Concorde. Yet Concorde exists in the ordinary physical world. There was no divine intervention which altered the laws of nature to favour Concorde. Its success has been achieved by the devotion of countless people who have been inspired by the concept. It ranks with the architectural marvels of the world – the Pyramids, the Gothic Cathedrals and the Taj Mahal.

This book was written to commemorate Concorde's first ten years in commercial service – from 21 January 1976 to 21 January 1986.

What follows is a brief description of some of the technical terms and concepts that the more inquisitive reader may find useful. In some instances these are expanded in the chapters that follow.

Ernst Mach*, an Austrian physicist, observed that airflows obeyed different laws as they approached the speed of sound. In recognition of his work, the term 'Mach number' was named after him. The Mach number of a moving body is the ratio of its speed to that of the speed of sound in the fluid in which it is travelling. The fluid in which aircraft travel is, of course, the air in the atmosphere. When an aircraft's speed is the same as the speed of sound it is said to have a Mach number of one – Mach 1.

Ernst Mach was a positivist who argued strongly against the notion that matter was made up of atoms. The explanation of why the airflow obeyed different laws, as the speed of sound is approached, is much easier to explain on the assumption that atoms and molecules exist. It is therefore curious that Mach did not agree with what has now become the accepted truth.

Air is a gas which is made up of molecules moving randomly at high speed. Their speed varies with temperature. They move more quickly when it is hot than when it is cold. The speed of sound in air is the speed at which vibrations or changes of pressure are transmitted through the air. As this speed is a function of the speed the molecules move,

sound travels quicker in hot air than in cold.

At 15°C (59°F), the average temperature found at sea level, the speed of sound is about 760 mph (660 knots). Between 50,000 ft and 60,000 ft, where the temperature averages minus 57°C (−71°F), it is 660 mph (573 knots). It varies in fact with the square root of absolute temperature (absolute zero is minus 273°C (−459.4°F) thus the freezing point of water is 273° Kelvin and its boiling point 373°K, etc).

An aircraft in flight can be travelling subsonically, i.e. below the speed of sound, or supersonically, i.e. above the speed of sound. The airflow, as Mach observed, is governed by two quite different laws depending on whether the aircraft is flying at subsonic or supersonic speeds. There is, however, a third definition of speed, and that is 'transonic'. In reality 'transonic' refers to a range of speeds typically from Mach 0.75 to Mach 1.3. It is called 'transonic' because both supersonic and subsonic (governed by their respective laws) are present simultaneously.

At first sight it is not obvious why a supersonic airflow can be present when an

*1838–1916.

The airspeed indicator on Concorde showing just over 500 knots, whilst the Machmeter indicates just less than Mach 2 corresponding to a true airspeed of 1,150 knots. The apparent discrepancy is due to the low density of the air found at 53,000 ft causing the aircraft to 'feel' only 500 knots. See the 'Flight envelope' on page 122

aircraft is flying subsonically. The reason is that an aircraft in flight separates the air. The airflow over the more bulbous parts of the aircraft (over a protruding cockpit or over the top of the wings) has to travel further than the air underneath the aircraft. Thus the air travelling the further distance over the aircraft has to travel more quickly. To be consistent with the law of energy conservation, as the 'moving' energy of the air increases, its pressure energy must reduce. Low pressure on the top surface of a wing sucks it upwards, or gives it 'lift'. When the speed of an aircraft exceeds about Mach 0.75 the faster moving air over the wings reaches Mach 1. Therefore supersonic airflow is found on an aircraft flying subsonically.

When the aircraft flies faster than Mach 1 some of the air, depending on the shape of the aircraft, is pulled along by the aircraft, so that part flows subsonically over the surface. Usually by the time the aircraft has reached about Mach 1.3 all the airflow over it is supersonic. Flight at transonic speeds was to prove more difficult than flight at supersonic speeds.

As an aircraft flies it experiences resistance from the air. This is known as 'drag'. The amount of lift compared to drag that an aircraft experiences at a given speed is a measure of its aerodynamic efficiency. This is known as the lift to drag ratio, commonly written as L/D. Drag is caused by the shape of the aircraft (form drag), by the surface of the aircraft (skin friction drag) and by the work the wings have to do to give lift (induced drag). The first two increase with speed, while induced drag decreases with speed.

At speeds below about 300 knots (1 knot = 1.15 mph), the airflow over an aircraft behaves like an incompressible fluid (like water). Above 300 knots the molecules of air, having had less 'warning' of the impending disturbance, become compressed. The 'warning' travels at the speed of sound. As the aircraft travels closer to Mach 1 the molecules have progressively less time in which to redistribute themselves before the passage of the aircraft. Now they build up and make, at Mach 1, a distinct 'compression wave' or 'shock wave'. This wave, analogous to a bow wave of a boat, increases the drag. Hence the notion that there was some kind of barrier at Mach 1, although projectiles like bullets had exceeded the speed of sound for over two hundred years. At the rear of an aircraft flying above Mach 1 is another compression wave where the air reverts to its original condition, having steadily reduced to a lower pressure during the passage of the aircraft. These two shock waves can usually be heard on the ground as a double boom.

At first sight it is difficult to visualise that

The shock waves formed in the air around a supersonic aircraft are analogous to the waves formed by a moving boat. Here water is flowing over a thin silhouette of Concorde to demonstrate the analogy. Although these waves are formed in just two dimensions, the shock waves on an aircraft are in three dimensions, forming a cone at the nose the air ahead of an object moving at subsonic speed starts to redistribute itself before the arrival of the object. Observation of light airborne objects, like snowflakes or thistle seeds, becoming wafted over the windscreen of a moving car demonstrates the effect. Heavier objects like grit and raindrops do not deflect. Should the car accelerate towards Mach 1, the deflection of even the light objects would not happen. Their first 'knowledge' of the car would be the car itself.

Once the sound barrier had been 'broken' another barrier appeared – the heat barrier. The faster an aircraft flies the more it is heated by the air which surrounds it. This is not an effect which is suddenly manifest, as it is present at all speeds, but does not become significant until the aircraft is travelling supersonically. It is caused by the compression of the air as it is accelerated during the passage of the aircraft. When any gas is compressed its temperature rises, as is readily observed when pumping up a

Wind tunnel models of Concorde were used to check its viability throughout the speed range. Here flight at slow speeds, requiring high angles of attack, is about to be investigated

bicycle tyre. The end of the pump becomes very hot due to the compression of the air within it. On an aircraft this effect is known as kinetic heating.

The temperature rise in degrees centigrade can be calculated approximately by squaring the true airspeed in mph of the aircraft and dividing this by 100. At Mach 2, about 1,320 mph, the rise is 174°C (345°F); at Mach 3 it is 392°C (737°F). These quantities are for the point experiencing the greatest temperature rise, usually the tip of the

aircraft's nose, where the air is accelerated to the speed of the aircraft. To this figure must be added the static air temperature. Above 37,000 ft this averages minus 57°C (−71°F), varying from place to place over the globe. At Mach 2 the final top temperature is thus 117°C (243°F) and at Mach 3 it is 335°C (635°F). Kinetic heating has an immense bearing on the choice of cruising speed for a supersonic transport aircraft (SST) and the materials from which it will be built. Aluminium alloys can easily cope with temperatures up to about 130°C (266°F); higher than that, more expensive titanium alloys must be used.

To monitor the temperature experienced by the nose of fast moving aircraft there is a gauge in the cockpit. It simply reads degrees centigrade. There are other instruments like the altimeter and compass which say, with a fair degree of accuracy, how high the aircraft is and in which direction it is pointing. There is one instrument, however, which to the untutored eye appears as if it is constantly telling a frightful lie (unless it is observed at sea level) and that is the airspeed indicator.

At sea level the speed shown on the airspeed indicator corresponds quite closely to the True Airspeed (TAS). But as the aircraft climbs into the thinner air the indicator registers an airspeed which is less than true. At Mach 2 and 55,000 ft the true airspeed would be 1,150 knots, but because of the low density of the air, the indicated airspeed is only 500 knots.

Aircraft are flown with special reference to indicated airspeed since this is a measure of what the aircraft feels. Knowledge of what the aircraft 'feels' tells the pilots how the aircraft can perform; how close it is, for instance, to losing the ability to give lift (stalling). Or, in the case of Concorde, how much extra thrust will be required to overcome the high induced drag when flying at landing speeds.

Indicated airspeed also shows the pilot how great an angle of attack the aircraft is experiencing. The angle of attack is the angle between the aircraft and the flow of air. As the speed falls so this angle increases, thus lift is maintained. If constant altitude is to be maintained during deceleration, the aircraft must be pitched up to compensate for the increased angle of attack. When descending to land, Concorde has quite a high pitch attitude (11°). This is because of the high angle of attack (14°) associated with low indicated airspeed.

The Background

The E28/39 or Gloster-Whittle. Britain's first jet propelled aircraft, which first flew 14 May 1941. Its engine gave a modest 850 lb of thrust. The engine planned for the US SST was to have given close on 70,000 lb of thrust

'Pull steadily, watch the altimeter, don't flap and don't expect anything much to happen until below 15,000 to 20,000 ft . . .' This advice was contained in a document written by George Bulman, Chief Test Pilot of Hawker Aircraft in 1943. It was intended for pilots who found themselves in aircraft diving at speeds close to that of sound.

A number of Allied fighter aircraft had experienced strange effects when diving at such speeds during the Second World War. Not the least of these effects had been the dangerous tendency for the controls to do the reverse of what was expected of them and for the whole aircraft to buffet and shake, sometimes to the point of structural failure. To preserve frontline fighter pilots and to investigate flight at speeds close to Mach 1 – thus forestalling any German advance in the new science – a series of high speed dives was planned.

The aircraft chosen for these investigations was the Photo Reconnaissance Spitfire (PR Mark XI) fitted with the Merlin 61 engine. Such a Spitfire was capable of climbing to 40,000 ft – high even by the standard of the subsonic jets of the mid-1980s. To achieve the highest speeds the power dive had to be started from as high as possible. For that and the reason of its relatively thin wings, the Spitfire PR Mark XI was considered a suitable aircraft for research into flight at transonic speed.

Some time in 1943, Squadron Leader Martindale, a test pilot for Rolls-Royce in civil life, found himself in a 45 degree dive from 40,000 ft. After 36 seconds from the start of the dive, descending through 29,000 ft, the Spitfire attained Mach 0.9. From about Mach 0.75 upwards some of the airflow became compressed and therefore subject to different aerodynamic laws. The Spitfire experienced increased drag, loss of lift and a tendency to pitch further nose down. Uncorrected the nose-down pitch would increase the dive angle. To prevent this the pilot would pull the stick back to apply 'up elevator'. At transonic speeds such action exposed the aircraft to another risk. Due to lack of stiffness in the tailplane and the great force of a compressed airstream on the up-going elevator, the leading edge of the tailplane could bend upwards leaving the elevator trailing in the slipstream. This resulted in the controls achieving the reverse effect of what was expected, namely pitching the aircraft further nose down. This effect is quite separate from the nose dropping due to the redistribution of the lift.

Entering the warmer atmosphere the Spitfire found itself in an environment where the speed of sound was greater. Although still travelling at roughly the same true airspeed, its speed with respect to the speed of sound (Mach number) was lower. The danger now was that the laws governing the airflow at the slower speeds would suddenly be restored. The 'up-elevator', which had maintained the dive angle could now, at the smaller Mach numbers, reassert itself with unnerving suddenness, pulling the aircraft out of the dive at such a rate that the wings might fold upwards, or flutter like a flag. There were no ejection seats in those days.

These investigations into flight at speeds close to Mach 1 would have been given immense publicity in peace-time. In the event they were cloaked in war-time secrecy and by the time the story was told, it appeared rather pedestrian compared to the rocket- and jet-propelled attempts on the sound barrier going on in the late 1940s. It is of lasting tribute to the Spitfire that it behaved better at such speeds than some of the later aircraft of supposedly more advanced aerodynamic design.

The Rolls-Royce Merlin 61 engine, which powered the PR XI, had been developed and fitted to the Spitfire Mark IX in response to a formidable new fighter fielded by the Germans in 1941: the Focke-Wulf 190. The increased performance of the Merlin 61 was largely due to the effectiveness of its supercharger. This added 70 mph to the top speed and 10,000 ft to the Spitfire's maximum altitude. In consequence it out-performed the Fock-Wulf 190.

A supercharger is a device that compress-es the air before it undergoes further compression in the cylinders of a piston engine. The supercharger on the Merlin 61 engine had been refined to near perfection by a brilliant young engineer at Rolls-Royce in Derby – Stanley Hooker.

Stanley Hooker (later Sir Stanley Hooker) had been recruited in 1938 by the works manager of Rolls-Royce Ernest W. Hives (later Lord Hives of Duffield) with the somewhat enigmatic words: 'You are not much of an engineer, are you?'! Hooker's work on superchargers was soon to have great relevance in the development of the jet engine, since the centrifugal compressors of the early jet engines were similar in principle to, although much larger than, the supercharger of the Merlin. The jet engine turned out to be the most suitable power plant for continuous supersonic flight. Eleven years after his work on the Merlin supercharger, Stanley Hooker began the transformation of the Bristol Olympus engine, destined, in its most superlative version, to power Concorde.

The 'barrier' to greater speed from the Spitfire during its transonic dive was due to two effects. One was the large increase of drag it experienced as the compression waves built up at Mach 0.9; the other was the loss of thrust experienced by the propeller. The combined effect of aircraft forward speed and the turning speed of the propeller ensured that the outer portions of the propeller blades were travelling at supersonic speeds. At such speeds the propeller becomes very inefficient. Thus the Spitfire lost thrust just as its drag increased. A rocket-propelled, rather than a gravity-assisted, Spitfire might have been able to maintain Mach 0.9 for longer.

Rocket propulsion has the advantage over other kinds of propulsion in that the thrust it generates is not dependent on the forward speed of the aircraft. Nor is its thrust dependent on altitude, if anything it increases as the pressure of air around it decreases. Although rocket-propelled air-craft are spared the need of having any kind of air intakes, they suffer the greater burden of having to carry extra fuel weight in the form of liquid oxygen (or some chemical suitable for combustion with the fuel). They therefore do not give propulsion suitable for sustained flight.

Happily by 1943 there had appeared an engine which looked capable of giving sustained thrust both at subsonic and supersonic speeds. This was the jet engine. This new engine gave thrust not through a propeller, but by virtue of its high speed jet efflux. The fact that its intake might be in a supersonic airflow would be, if anything, a bonus, since the incoming air could be slowed down and therefore 'supercharged'

The Rolls-Royce Merlin engine of a Spitfire, showing the circular supercharger casing to the rear. Stanley Hooker's work on the supercharger transformed the performance of this engine; later he was to transform the Bristol Olympus jet engine

prior to entering the compressor on the engine, making the engine yet more efficient.

The inventor of the jet engine principle, Sir Frank Whittle, said that he was regarded at the time as a crazy optimist. One of his early proposals (in 1935), envisaged an engine giving 111 lb of thrust to a 2000 lb aircraft travelling at 500 mph at an altitude of 69,000 ft. It is anyone's guess what people would have said had he predicted that a 350,000 lb aircraft (including the fuel) would be capable of travelling at 1,320 mph at 55,000 ft with each of its four engines giving, at that altitude, 10,000 lb of thrust.

Jet-propelled flight became a reality in Britain in 1941 with the first flight of the Gloster-Whittle (E28/39). A Whittle engine, the Power Jets W2/700, was chosen, in 1943, as the power plant for Britain's first supersonic project: the Miles M52 (E24/43). It was hoped optimistically that the M52 would exceed 1,000 mph (about Mach 1.5) in level flight. There was a great deal of controversy over the choice of wing section for the aircraft. Thin wings, suitable for supersonic flight, seemed to be the obvious choice, but their lack of efficiency at subsonic speeds meant that the aircraft would not be able to climb to such a high altitude as one fitted with conventional

wings. The higher the altitude, the higher the Mach number that could be attained in the ensuing dive. Once comfortably supersonic it was hoped that the aircraft could level off maintaining speed – engine thrust having increased to cope with the higher drag associated with supersonic flight.

The W2/700 was one of the last engines built by the Power Jets Company. Under the leadership of Frank Whittle, a small and dedicated team working in appallingly primitive surroundings near Rugby in England (Sir Stanley Hooker referred to them as Whittle's rabbit hutch) had researched, designed and built a viable jet engine. After an unsatisfactory period of liaison with the Rover company, Rolls-Royce became involved with Power Jets and, under the leadership of Stanley Hooker, set about developing and producing the jet engine in quantity.

The lineage of the modern jet engine owes far more to the early British engines than to the jet engines developed in Germany. On observing the immense length of runway required by the Me 262 (the German jet-powered fighter) on take-off, an onlooker remarked to Frank Whittle, who was also present, that it was no wonder that Hitler wanted to extend the Third Reich.

Soon it became evident that more research was needed to give sufficient thrust to the M52. The reason that the Ministry of Supply gave for the cancellation of the project in 1946, however, was that they were concerned for the safety of its pilot. In 1948, a pilotless, rocket-propelled, scaled down version of the M52 did achieve about Mach 1.4, which proved that its planform with straight wings could cope with supersonic flight. However, at the end of the Second World War, British design was influenced by swept wings which gave better performance at both supersonic and high subsonic speeds.

Before the outbreak of the Second World War a German scientist, Professor Adolf Büsemann, had published findings that suggested that swept wings would perform better than straight wings in supersonic flight. One significant reason for this is that the shock waves generated at the nose of an aircraft miss the wing tips if these are swept back. Thus there is not the added complication of an interference between wings and shock waves. Astonishingly these findings, freely available to all, went unnoticed.

Equally remarkable was the failure of the Allies to understand why the wings were swept on the rocket-propelled German fighter (the Messerschmitt Me 163 – Komet). The Komet was a tailless swept-winged interceptor, which was very fast, achieving Mach 0.8 (about 550 mph) for short periods. The Allies believed that its speed could be ascribed to its being rocket-propelled. The reason for the swept wings was thought to be so that adequate control could be retained in pitch (the control of the longitudinal angle of the fuselage about itself). Though both beliefs were partly correct, what was not understood was that swept wings allowed the aircraft to fly at speeds closer to Mach 1, since the increase in drag was delayed until these higher speeds were reached.

From the description of the Spitfire tests, it will be remembered that some of the air becomes supersonic over an aircraft even though that aircraft is travelling subsonically. It is the portion of the supersonic airflow which causes the drag rise.

Thick wings experience this transonic drag rise at lower Mach numbers than thin wings. Wings must support the weight of the aircraft and have within them some space to contain fuel. High speed aircraft need both strength and as much space for fuel as possible. The conflict can be resolved

The Me 163B Komet, Germany's rocket-propelled interceptor. Note the absence of a tailplane. Rocket propulsion was available for 8 to 10 minutes, giving speeds in excess of 550 mph. Its swept wings allowed flight at high subsonic Mach numbers before the transonic drag rise took effect. The planform of the D.H. 108 was somewhat similar to this aircraft by sweeping the wings either forward or back. Although the ratio of the thickness of the wing to the distance from leading to trailing edge remains constant, the sweep-back makes this ratio 'appear' smaller to the airflow. Now the air is less disturbed by the passage of the aircraft, so the aircraft can fly faster before the compression waves start to apply their drag increase. The benefit of this discovery, made by Professor Albert Betz (a German aerodynamicist), has been applied to jet-propelled airliners, virtually all of which have swept back wings.

To research flight with a swept-winged aircraft, the de Havilland company modified a Vampire, a single engined, straight-winged fighter, with its tail and fin surfaces connected via twin booms to the wings. The booms and the tail surface were removed, swept back wings fitted, and a swept fin was placed over the rear end of the fuselage. It resembled the Komet in many outward respects. The DH108 was partly intended as a research aircraft for what became the Comet airliner. At that time the philosophy among several British aircraft manufac-turers had been that it was desirable to perfect a 'flying wing' to reduce the aerodynamic drag and the extra weight caused by tailplane surfaces. Sadly, after the loss of several such aircraft, to lack of control in pitch, this philosophy had to be abandoned.

'Flying wings', as tailless aircraft were dubbed, would have had to carry their payload within the wing. For people to stand inside the wing it would have had to have been at least 7 ft thick. The wing span would have been huge to cope with such a thickness. Furthermore without a tailplane there was no way of aerodynamically balancing wing flaps. Without flaps either the landing speed would have had to have been very fast or the wing too big for efficient cruise. It would thus have been an uneconomic proposition – the de Havilland Comet had a tail!

Two other British aircraft design philo-sophies had their origins in the immediate post-war era. One was to produce a wing capable of sustaining laminar flow. Hitherto the flow of air over a wing had always been impeded by that little turbulent layer of air close to the wing known as the boundary layer. Laminar flow control promised a very marked reduction in aerodynamic drag.

The other philosophy was the notion that the aerodynamic drag associated with the engines and intakes could be reduced by placing the engine air intakes at the wing roots feeding air to engines that were 'buried', as on the Comet 4, rather than podded, as on the Boeing 707.

The laminar flow concept failed largely because it seemed impossible to retain a completely clean wing. Even a squashed insect, acquired during take-off, upset the laminar flow. Removal of the boundary layer

The D.H. 108, Britain's first transonic swept winged aircraft. Control in roll and pitch on aircraft without tailplanes has to be achieved through the surfaces on the trailing edge of the wing. John Derry exceeded the speed of sound in this aircraft (VW 120)–the first British aircraft to do so

The de Havilland
Comet 1, Britain's
great leap forward in
the post-war aviation
era. Stresses at the
right angular corners
of the windows were
higher than
predicted; hence the
metal fatigue that led
to fatal crashes. But
for the accidents de
Havilland might have
retained their world
lead in jet airliner
construction

through minute holes drilled in the surface of the wing was another solution, though rather impractical, at least in those days. However, laminar flow control was put forward again in the mid-1980s as a means of reducing drag on an Advanced Supersonic Transport (AST).

The presence of a boundary layer can be readily observed on a car windscreen during rain. Even when driving at 70 mph the smaller drops remain stationary. The larger ones which protrude out of the boundary layer are moved by the airstream but not that quickly. It is some millimetres away from the screen that the speed of the airstream assumes its expected value.

Although the concept of buried engines worked, it was not such a satisfactory answer to the drag and weight problem as the solution developed by the Americans. For their 707, Boeing placed their engines in pods slung beneath and slightly ahead of the wing, on pylons. The engine intakes benefitted from a clean airflow not disturbed by the unpredictable behaviour at the junction of wing and fuselage. Furthermore the distribution of the engine weight to the wings meant that this part of the total weight did not have to be borne through the wing root. Thus this part was lighter too.

The de Havilland
Comet 4. The
windows have
rounded corners
following experience
with the Comet 1.
The engines are
buried at the wing
roots—a philosophy
preferred in Britain to
the underslung pods
chosen by Boeing and
other US
manufacturers. The
pods outboard on the
wings are fuel tanks

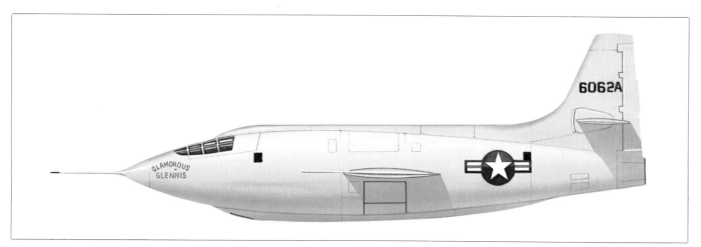

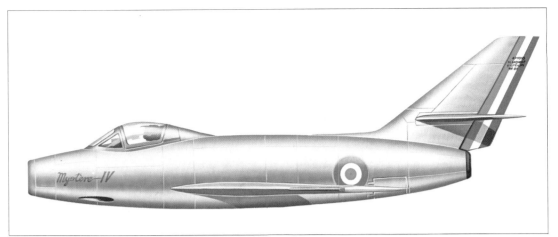

This advantage does not favour aircraft with rear fuselage mounted engines.

In 1948, John Derry, Chief Test Pilot of de Havilland, became, more by accident than by design, the first pilot in Britain to exceed Mach 1, in a DH108 during a test flight investigating transonic flight. Whilst attempting to recover from a dive at Mach 0.97, his aeroplane exceeded the vertical and achieved Mach 1.02. He was lucky to survive. Geoffrey de Havilland Jnr, son of the founder of the firm had been killed in a DH108 almost exactly two years earlier probably having experienced similar very severe oscillations in pitch.

By the early 1950s data had been acquired which would make the next steps in supersonic flight slightly easier. The first aim then was to build a jet fighter capable of intercepting the mammoth Russian nuclear bombers which were under development, and were capable of cruising between 30,000 and 40,000 ft at around Mach 0.8.

The fighter had to have an excellent rate of climb and at least double the bomber's speed for a successful interception long before the bomber could reach its target. The second aim was to build a supersonic bomber which, because of its speed, would itself be very difficult to intercept.

Long range supersonic flight, however, was going to be much more difficult to achieve than the short duration dash required of an interceptor. But should a bomber become a reality then a transport derivative could follow, such was the pattern generally established during the 50 years of aircraft development. But as far as the development of an SST was concerned, the introduction of missiles even capable of intercepting supersonic bombers at high altitude was to upset this evolutionary pattern. The SST would have to be developed almost in its own right.

The Formative Phase

The Fairey Delta 2. Fairey believed that the delta wing with no tail was the optimum solution for a supersonic aircraft. Peter Twiss achieved a new world air speed record of 1,132 mph in the FD2 in March 1956. Another version of the FD2 (BAC 221) appeared with wings modified to the 'Ogee' planform to research separated airflow on an aircraft with a greater speed range than the HP 115 for the Concorde project

Prompted by the preponderance of designs for supersonic interceptor aircraft that appeared in the early 1950s people began to wonder whether a civil supersonic transport (SST) could one day be a possibility. With London to New York flight times being of the order of 18 hours and more, especially against headwinds and with refuelling stops, the idea of doing the same journey in a fifth of the time must have seemed preposterous.

Nevertheless Sir Arnold Hall, director of the Royal Aircraft Establishment (RAE) Farnborough in the early 1950s, asked Morien Morgan, already involved with the Advanced Fighter Project Group, to chair a small committee to look into the possibility of building a civil supersonic transport. The reported findings, in 1954, suggested that it

might just be possible to fly 15 passengers from London to New York at Mach 2 in an aircraft with an all up weight of 300,000 lb (136,000 kg). For comparison Concorde carries 100 passengers (up to 128 with reduced space between seat rows) over that range with an all up weight (maximum take-off weight including the passengers and the fuel) of 408,000 lb (185,000 kg). The envisaged 15-seater SST was based on the design of the Avro 730 supersonic bomber project that was cancelled in 1957. It had thin unswept wings with engines mounted on the wing tips. But for an SST to be economically viable, a better aerodynamic shape would have to be devised.

Such a shape did appear with dramatic impact, in the form of the British Fairey Delta 2. On 10 March 1956 Peter Twiss

(Chief Test Pilot of Fairey Aviation) exceeded the previous world airspeed record, held by the American Col. Haynes in a F100 Super Sabre, by the handsome margin of 310 mph. A reheated Rolls-Royce Avon RA5 turbojet propelled the FD2 at the astonishing speed of 1,132 mph (Mach 1.7).

In November 1956 the Supersonic Transport Aircraft Committee (STAC) was formed, chaired by Morien Morgan, one of the greatest proponents for civil supersonic flight. Hearing evidence from 17 interested bodies, comprising the aircraft industry, airlines and ministries, its conclusions were reported in 1959. The result was Concorde which ten years later made its maiden flight.

Contributors to its success were the FD2 and the P1, both offsprings of Morien Morgan's Advanced Fighter Project group which had been formed in 1948. The success of these two aircraft banished the notion of some kind of intractable barrier at Mach 1, the speed of sound. It is interesting to look at the different design philosophies.

Both designers produced a different planform: the P1 with swept wings and a tailplane, while the FD2 a delta wing without a tail. Tailless designs had encountered many problems, as exemplified by Geoffrey de Havilland's experience in the DH108, hence English Electric wanted to ensure stability and control through use of a

tail surface, especially for flight in the tricky transonic range. Fairey believed, however, that a 60 degree delta with powerful trailing edge control surfaces would provide a stable aircraft throughout this range. After all, experience had pointed to the fact that tail surfaces were a major source of aerodynamic buffet at transonic speeds – why run this risk by having a tail at all?

As it turned out both designs were supremely successful. In different ways both contributed to Concorde's eventual success: the FD2, because it was converted into the modified delta shape that was to be applied to Concorde; the P1, because a great deal was learned about the variable exhaust nozzle on the Rolls-Royce Avon engine, a necessary device for the efficient use of a variable thrust reheat system. It is the variable exhaust nozzle system on the Olympus engine, as fitted to Concorde, which ekes out every last remaining ounce of thrust and fuel economy from the jet efflux both with and without reheat.

'Reheat', or 'after-burner' as it is known in the United States, is a device which can be fitted to the rear of the main jet engine, within the exhaust duct, to give an extra 'push' to the aircraft. It consists of a ring from which fuel may be burned in the engine exhaust gases, which still has sufficient oxygen in it to support combustion, prior to

P1 Lightning. The tail surface can be clearly seen. The English Electric designers considered that inclusion of a tail would give the stability and control required for supersonic flight provided it was positioned away from the wake of the wing. The exhaust nozzles of the two Avon engines are mounted one above the other. The nozzles could vary the area of the exit orifice—wide open with full reheat in use, and diminishing with intermediate amounts of reheat. Perfection of variable jet nozzles was essential before a commercial SST could become a reality

The buckets or secondary nozzles on Concorde. The left-hand picture shows the nozzle in its divergent position as it would be in supersonic flight. The right-hand picture shows the nozzle as it would be for take-off, the gap allowing ambient air to break up the boundary to the jet efflux making it less noisy. For their position to give reverse thrust, see page 104

Opposite, top Sir Barnes Wallis with a model of Swallow. Although the cockpit and undercarriage have been extended for this photograph the wings are in the fully swept position for supersonic flight – a combination that would not have been found in practice. Surrounding Sir Barnes are examples of his earlier engineering efforts including bombs, airships, the Wellington bomber and geodetic construction

Inset A polymorphous photograph of Swallow showing the extent of the variable geometry. Note that the engine pairs on the wingtips were to have been hinged. There was no fin

*See appendix.

its leaving via the exhaust nozzle. As the velocity of the jet efflux is so much greater with reheat on, the exhaust nozzle must vary in area to accommodate two situations. On the FD2 the reheat was either on or off, thus the exhaust nozzle only had the two positions – wide open or open. On the P1 the reheat was variable so the exhaust nozzle had to be variable as well. On the Olympus 593, as fitted to Concorde, not only is there a variable nozzle to accommodate the reheat, but there is a secondary nozzle which, amongst other things, forms a divergent duct for efficiency during the supersonic cruise. Furthermore the primary nozzle area varies continually, even without reheat, thus keeping the Olympus engine constantly in tune*.

The Supersonic Transport Aircraft Committee (STAC) met regularly from November 1956 until March 1959. Among its recommendations was one which strongly favoured building a long-range SST to carry 150 passengers from London to New York non-stop with a cruising speed of not less than Mach 1.8. There was also a recommendation for the construction of a shorter range SST to cruise at Mach 1.2. The committee regarded cruising speeds approaching Mach 3 as feasible, but technically difficult due to the heating effect discussed in the Preface. At Mach 3 the highest temperature experienced by the fuselage is around 335°C (635°F) thus not only is it much more difficult to keep the occupants cool, but the skin has to be made from the more expensive alloys of titanium and perhaps even from stainless steel. The cheaper and

well tested aluminium alloy, although highly satisfactory at temperatures up to 130°C (265°F), does not cope with temperatures of over 300°C (572°F) at all. A Mach 3 version was regarded by the STAC as a possible second generation SST.

Between London and New York a cruising speed of Mach 3, compared to Mach 2, would reduce the total journey time by about 40 minutes, about 20 per cent. The real gain of a Mach 2 airliner was that it could more than double the speed of the current subsonic airliners, which were designed to cruise at just above Mach 0.8. Any economic gains associated with the yet quicker journey times made possible at a speed of Mach 3 would be more than wiped out by the fact that a Mach 3 SST would cost disproportionally more to build. Development costs were put at £75–£95m for the Mach 1.8 SST and £50–£80m for the slower shorter range versions, at 1959 values. It was considered that they would cost about 50 per cent more to operate than a similarly-sized subsonic aircraft.

Following the recommendations of the STAC, feasibility studies were commissioned by the Ministry of Defence, then headed by Duncan Sandys. Bristol produced studies of an SST with a conventional fuselage and slender delta wings, but Hawker Siddeley provided a study for an integral layout – a slender delta with a longitudinal swelling in which would be housed the passengers – virtually a slender delta flying wing.

Duncan Sandys' somewhat infamous defence White Paper in 1957 had put a temporary halt to the development of manned military aircraft in Britain (including the Avro 730 supersonic bomber) in favour of missiles. So a rather stunned aircraft industry must have welcomed the opportunity to research and possibly build an SST. By 1959, when Duncan Sandys had commissioned the feasibility studies for an SST, plans for the new British Supersonic Tactical Strike Reconnaissance Aircraft – the TSR2 – had been unveiled. However, in 1966 Britain's Labour government cancelled – among other aircraft – the TSR2. To quote Sir Stanley Hooker on British military aviation policy: 'We were in, we were out, then we were in again and finally out. It was more like a boat race than a policy.'

Among other designs which were also put forward at about this time was the Barnes Wallis Swallow. This consisted of an aircraft in which variable sweep had been taken to the extreme. The engines, outboard on the wings, were hinged and could be used for stability and control in place of aerodynamic surfaces. Furthermore their movement with the wing sweep contributed to the balance of the aircraft. Concorde retains aerodynamic balance at different speeds by moving the fuel to change the centre of gravity.

An 'arrow' planform is attractive because it is very efficient aerodynamically at supersonic speeds. To keep the drag down on Swallow, the pilots would have had a retractable cockpit. Studies for advanced supersonic transports make use of the 'arrow' planform; but without recourse to variable geometry, the 'arrow' cannot be so marked as the one on Swallow. In the un-

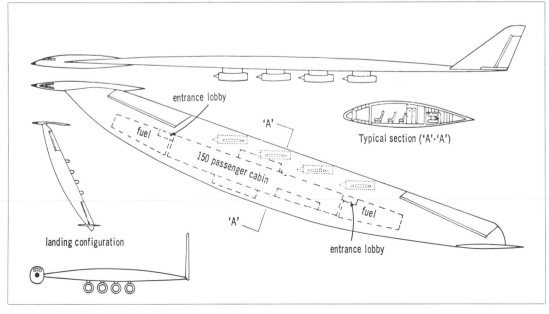

entrance lobby

fuel

150 passenger cabin

'A'

'A'

fuel

entrance lobby

landing configuration

Typical section ('A'-'A')

The slewed-wing proposal from Handley Page. Runways would have had to have taken on different proportions if this 1961 idea had taken root!

A Concorde taking off from runway 31L (left hand of the two northwest facing runways) at Kennedy, New York. The reheats (afterburners) are in use. The volume of low pressure over the wings (giving 170 tonnes of lift) can be seen clearly, in the form of the condensation that has formed in the damp atmosphere

swept arrangement, the engines on Swallow were very far from the centre-line. This would have given the pilots quite a control problem following an engine failure. In spite of Sir Barnes Wallis' original thinking, it might have been difficult to make the arrangement work without the electronic techniques available in the 1980s. Boeing's main study for an SST (the Boeing 2707-200) proposed using variable geometry, but with the engines fixed beneath the tailplane.

Another quite revolutionary and somewhat odd looking proposal was for the Handley Page slewed wing. Although lift to drag ratios (L/D) are good in theory with such an arrangement, the control problem looked extremely complicated. However, it too would have benefitted from the digital computors of the 1980s. A slewed wing aircraft with fixed fuselage is under development at NASA in the USA. Nevertheless this still appears a rather unlikely solution to the problem of how to design an SST.

A third proposal envisaged a slender delta with a large number of lifting engines to give it a vertical take-off capability. No less than fifty such engines were thought to be necessary on a transatlantic SST! The rate of fuel burn of the lifting engines was

expected to be very high – and the result of them all failing to start simultaneously prior to landing would have left the aircraft in a somewhat dangerous state.

These three proposals (and the Boeing 2707-200) failed to exploit the discovery that extra lift could be obtained by allowing the airflow to separate over the upper surface of a slender delta wing. To give lift, under normal circumstances, the flow of air over a wing must not separate from the wing. The airflow travels slightly further over the top surface than under the bottom surface and so has to move more quickly over the top than the bottom. As it accelerates its pressure drops. In this way the wing is 'sucked' upwards, rendering lift to it and to whatever the wing is attached. Should this airflow become turbulent, thus breaking away from its ordered flow, the lift will suddenly reduce; the wing is then said to 'stall'. At the tip of a wing in normal flight is a small vortex – a kind of horizontal whirlpool of air caused by the higher pressure air underneath spilling over into the lower pressure air on top, an effect which can be highlighted by the use of smoke in a wind tunnel (it is somewhat akin to the whirlpool seen over the plug of an emptying bath). Such a vortex, on a larger scale, can be harnessed to give extra lift to a slender delta wing in slow speed flight.

A big contribution in the study of flow separation was made by E. C. Maskell of RAE. He and the late Dr Dietrich Küchemann, head of Aerodynamics at RAE and a German Second World War scientist 'inherited' by Britain, laid the foundations of this new technique.

Furthermore, the slender delta wing behaved very satisfactorily during transonic and supersonic flight. This was the breakthrough – the discovery of a planform which theoretically could remain unaltered throughout a vast speed range. There would be no need to fit flaps and slats, which add so much to the weight and complexity of conventional airliners. A practical test was needed to prove both that the theory was correct and that no dangerous side effects would prevent it being applied to an SST.

Consequently the feasibility programme that was commissioned following the final report from STAC, included a contract to Handley Page to build an aircraft to test what the flying paper darts, beloved by schoolboys, had suggested: that vortex lift could give sufficiently stable lift to allow a slender delta flying at low speed to be controllable.

The resulting aircraft was the experimental Handley Page 115. It was powered by a single Viper jet engine. Although its 76 degree swept wings gave the illusion that it was built for great speed it was designed purely to explore flight at low speeds – it did not even have a retractable undercarriage.

The handling of the HP 115 was better than anyone had dared to hope. It gave excellent lift at slow speed. Even landing in a cross-wind, a situation which might have caused difficulty, was trouble-free.

Success with the Handley Page 115 proved that the resulting SST would not have to be lumbered with flaps and slats to enable its wing to give sufficient lift at take-off and landing speeds. If it had one small vice it was that as the speed became slower the drag caused by the wings giving lift became greater. Although this obviates the need for air-brakes, the extra drag has to be overcome by increasing the thrust. Provided there is plenty of thrust available, all is well; but the danger lay in the pilot not spotting the speed loss and thus not applying the extra thrust required by the lower speed. Without proper monitoring of the speed it could fall off to the point, not of the wings being unable to give lift and so stalling, but

to the point where there was not enough thrust to overcome the extra drag associated with the low speed. To overcome this problem it was recognised that such an aircraft would have to be fitted with an automatic throttle. Indeed on Concorde there is just such a device and it works extremely well too. However, Concorde is surprisingly easy to fly in the very rare event of the auto-throttle not being available.

Although the slender delta promised to have a better lift to drag ratio (L/D) at supersonic speeds than other planforms the

Before the main landing gear can be retracted it has to be shortened so that it can fit into the undercarriage bays

Shock waves around a wind tunnel model of Concorde. The shock waves are three dimensional forming a cone at the nose. Compare these with the two dimensional ones generated around the Concorde silhouette model with a flow of water shown on page 9

The HP 115 in flight near Farnborough. This slender delta aircraft proved that a separated airflow could give lift at slow speeds. It first flew in August 1961. Its success paved the way for Concorde by showing that complex high lift devices for slow speed flight would not be necessary for slender deltas

unpalatable fact remains that there is a drag rise as Mach 1 is exceeded. In fact the L/D drops, on Concorde, from about 12 at Mach 0.95 to 7.5 at Mach 2. How then was the future SST going to have enough range to cross the Atlantic?

Happily jet-engine efficiency can be designed to improve with speed, more than compensating for the loss of aerodynamic efficiency. The projected SST was expected therefore to travel further (or at least as far) on a gallon of fuel at its supersonic cruising speed as it could at its subsonic cruising speed, expected to be in excess of Mach 0.9. This fortunate state of affairs is brought about because the efficiency of the turbojet engine is very much enhanced if the air is precompressed prior to engine entry. At speeds in excess of Mach 1.4 sufficient precompression can be arranged to occur inside the intake system where the air is slowed – hence compressed – to about half

The turboprop Vickers Viscount, the one post-war British civil aircraft that achieved a great commercial success. More than 400 were sold. The long-haul market however remained dominated by American aircraft

the speed of sound before it reaches the engine. Nobody doubted that the intake system would need some kind of variable 'throat' so that it could cope efficiently with various speeds and especially those in excess of Mach 1.5. Since engine efficiency improves with speed up to Mach 3, there was a great incentive to go as fast as the kinetic heating of the structure would allow – Mach 2.2 appeared the most attractive speed if a well-tried and tested aluminium alloy were used.

However, Mach 2.04, which reduced the maximum temperature from 156°C to 127°C (313°F to 261°F), was ultimately chosen since the lower temperature gave less of a problem with the oil and fuel.

By the late 1950s, it was realised, tantalisingly, that aerodynamic and thermo-dynamic development had progressed far enough to allow an SST to become a reality. The question now became: would disappointments with the performance of British civil aviation spur Government and Industry into turning the theory of a paper dart into a practical SST?

British civil aviation in the years after the Second World War had hoped to equal or better anything the Americans could produce. It was true that two major projects had been abandoned – the Princess Flying Boat and the Bristol Brabazon. But on the credit side the pure jet de Havilland Comet 1 and the turbo-prop Vickers Viscount were about to appear. At Bristol another potential world beater, the turbo-prop Britannia was also taking shape.

The Britannia, it was hoped, would replace most long-range piston-propelled airliners. The engine chosen to power the Britannia was the Proteus. Originally designed to fit within the wing of the Brabazon, it had an air intake arrangement which caused the air to turn through 180 degrees before entering the engine. At 20,000 ft in the moist air found over the tropics ice formed at the 180 degree elbow causing the engine to flameout (stop) on an early Britannia. Fears of a similar, if not worse problem over the Atlantic brought matters to a head. However, the moisture content over the Atlantic at 20,000 ft is not nearly as great as it is over the tropics. According to Sir Stanley Hooker a relatively easy modification would have sufficed. Nevertheless for worldwide operations a total cure had to be found. In the end a system of igniter plugs solved the problem and BOAC accepted the Britannia – some two years late – and just in time to be overtaken by the jets on the North Atlantic, notably the Boeing 707. Instead of 180 only 80 Britannias were sold, and a jet-powered version of the Britannia was beyond the

Opposite The number 4 engine intake on a Concorde. The two moveable 'ramps' can be clearly seen inside the top of the box. The extent of the movement on the forward one (labelled 'DO NOT USE . . .') can be clearly seen on the vertical dividing wall between this intake and its neighbour (to the right of this picture) in the form of 'rubbing' marks. Correct positioning of the ramps to focus the shock wave on the intake's lower lip was fundamental to engine efficiency in supersonic flight. During subsonic flight the ramps are raised, as shown here

The Bristol Britannia. The big British hope of the 1950s. Icing problems on the Bristol Proteus engines delayed its entry into service. Too soon it was overtaken by the long-range jet airliners. Its sales were further jeopardised by the appearance of the Vickers Vanguard—another four-engined turboprop airliner of similar size

resources of Bristol. On top of this, the British Aircraft Industry, lacking direction, had been allowed to build a competitor to the Britannia, the turbo-prop Vanguard. Each whittled down the sales of the other.

The designers of the medium-range jet-powered Comet 4 had, by 1958, overcome the devastating problem experienced with its direct forerunner the Comet 1. The corners of the windows had not been made strong enough to withstand metal fatigue with the result that three Comet 1s had experienced explosive decompression in flight. This salutary lesson caused the designers of Concorde to proceed with caution in every field and not least in the area of aircraft structure. The Comet 4 inaugurated the first transatlantic jet passenger service in October 1958 – two weeks before the Boeing 707.

It had been galling for Sir George Edwards, Chairman of Vickers, that BOAC had been allowed, by the British Government, to purchase the Boeing 707 from America in 1956. In the previous year, BOAC

and the RAF had turned down the British equivalent to the 707 – the Vickers VC7 (V-1000 in its military form). Based on the Vickers Valiant bomber, it had engines buried in the inboard section of the wing with intakes at the wing roots. The VC7 was scrapped, to be replaced by the Vickers VC10.

The Vickers VC10, with its clean wing and four rear-mounted engines, was originally conceived as an airliner capable of operating from high altitude airfields on hot days over the old 'empire' routes. Later its range was increased to compete with the Boeing 707. Although it was beloved by passengers as soon as it appeared in 1962, it was too late to sell in large quantities – the Boeing 707 had got in first. It typified the frightful dichotomy into which the relationship between the British Government, the nationalised carriers (BOAC and BEA) and the airline industry had fallen. The Government, according to Sir Basil Small-piece (Managing Director of BOAC from 1956–1963), had expected BOAC to support the British Aircraft Industry by buying British aircraft it did not want and then having to bear some of the financial burden incurred during the final stages of the development of the new aircraft. At the same time BOAC was expected to pay the Government a fixed rate of interest on the capital borrowed. It was galling to BOAC that a large quantity of that capital, in 1957, had had to be spent on acquiring 10 DC7Cs to fill the gap caused by the late delivery of the Britannia 312. Thus BOAC regarded the VC10 with a great deal of caution, fearing that the Government would force them to have a large number of VC10s they simply did not want. In the end some kind of compromise was reached, but not without acrimony.

Forewarned is forearmed. Sir Basil Small-peice and Sir Matthew Slattery of BOAC made it very clear to the British Government in 1960 that although they would be delighted to assist with any future SST, this would be at no financial risk to the airline and no orders would be placed unless the SST made economic sense. In the end the Government agreed to underwrite that risk.

It is true that there had been one British success – the short-haul Vickers Viscount, with sales exceeding 400. However, by the late 1950s and early 1960s, in the words of Sir Stanley Hooker, 'We've lost in the civil market to the Americans. Now these Boeing 707s and DC8s cannot possibly last for more than about ten years. Therefore in order to collar our fair share we must look towards building a supersonic airliner with a European partner.'

A Douglas DC-7C. This aircraft of the mid-1950s represented the peak of the piston-engined propeller-driven airliner development. The turboprop Britannia would have easily eclipsed it, had it not been overtaken by the Boeing 707

Agreement with France

British and French Concordes in formation. Each country operated the Concordes it had assembled. The Air France Concorde is shown in the pre-1976 livery

By 1961, Britain had convinced herself that it was both highly desirable and technically possible to build an Atlantic range (3,700 statute miles) SST. There was one piece of the jigsaw missing, however; could a suitable partner be found to share the large cost of such a project? The right choice of partner, it was hoped, would lead not only to a successful SST but to co-operation in a host of other fields. A European partner, for instance, might pave the way for Britain's entry into the Common Market. At that time Russia and America were pouring millions

into the exploration of space, without, apart from technical advance, any prospect of financial return. An SST promised technical advance and a financial return, the latter largely on the grounds that speed had always attracted customers.

Partnership with an American company was considered. But the Americans were more interested in Mach 3 designs. Such speeds had already been ruled out by the British designers on account of the kinetic heating problem.

The only European country with the

ability to undertake such a project in the early 1960s was France. France had had to rebuild its once proud aircraft industry from the ashes of the Second World War. She was, in 1960, one of the few nations – with

Russia, the United States, Sweden, Britain and Canada – to have designed, built and tested supersonic aircraft. Nevertheless the French Aircraft Industry would benefit enormously from Britain's technical know-how which had been enhanced rather than destroyed by the Second World War. As it turned out, Britain was to benefit from France's determination to see the project through.

Starting with the straight-winged Trident, first flown in 1953, France had built a series of supersonic research aircraft. It was the Trident which on one occasion caused some concern in the echelons of the British Radar Warning System. Charles Burnet (BAe Weybridge) who witnessed the incident said: 'One evening in the late 1950s a worried controller phoned Boscombe Down to find out if there were any test aircraft airborne from there at that time. Apparently a target had been detected flying down the Channel from the *east* at over 1,000 mph – it turned out to be the French Trident!' This aircraft was powered by two wing tip-mounted turbojets and a rocket unit in the fuselage.

After this came the delta-winged Gerfault which was capable, in 1954, of exceeding Mach 1 by use of a turbojet alone – without reheat or rocket assistance. But most spectacular of the French research aircraft was the Nord Griffon. It had a propulsion unit which consisted of a turbojet within a huge outer casing. This outer casing formed a ramjet. The turbojet engine was used for slow speed flight and for starting the ramjet. The Griffon achieved Mach 1.85 in 1957 (about 1,240 mph).

Ramjets work on the principle that due to the high forward speed, usually above Mach 1.5, there is sufficient natural compression of the air to supplant the rotating compressor of a turbojet. No compressor means no need for a turbine to drive the compressor hence no moving parts. Air entering the intake becomes compressed, is then heated by the burning fuel giving thrust to the engine as it accelerates out of the propelling nozzle. A ramjet does not give efficient propulsion until speeds of around Mach 4 are reached.

Many missiles are propelled by ramjets, but only once they have achieved a suitable speed, usually gained from a rocket engine. Concorde travels too slowly to benefit from ramjet propulsion.

On the civil side the French had some success with the subsonic twin-engined Sud-Est Caravelle airliner. Its nose section was in fact the same as the British de Havilland Comet's. There was a lot of collaboration. Incidentally Concorde was to inherit, via this lineage, the triple hydraulic system labelled blue, green and, as a backup, yellow, which was originally fitted to the Comet.

Concurrent with the Nord Griffon were the swept-winged Mysteres and the delta-winged Mirage fighters. The next logical step for Sud Aviation, as it had become by 1961, was to investigate the possibility of

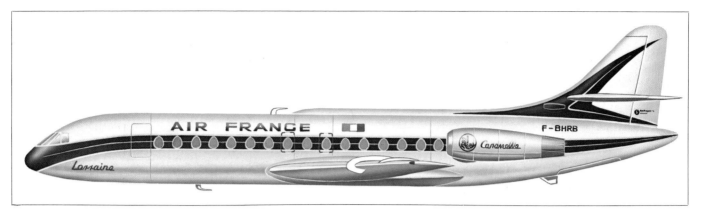

The Sud Aviation Caravelle. This successful French airliner had two rear-mounted engines. The nose owed its lines to the de Havilland Comet, as can be clearly seen

building an SST. Sud Aviation had been formed from Sud-Est, run by George Hereil, the original proposer of the Caravelle, and Sud Ouest.

Accordingly, at the Paris Air Show of June 1961 there appeared a model of a slender delta SST called the Super Caravelle. Although never built, it was designed to carry a payload of 70 passengers over 2,000 miles.

The Super Caravelle was thus not to have transatlantic range. In fact there was to be some wrangling between the British and French over this question of range. The British, in spite of a mild flirtation with an 'M-winged' medium range Mach 1.2 aircraft, had never considered it worthwhile to build anything with less range than London (or Paris) to New York. The Super Caravelle bore a remarkable resemblance to the BAC 223, the latest proposal from Archibald Russell, technical director of Bristol Aircraft which, by late 1961, had become part of the British Aircraft Corporation (BAC). (Included in the merger were Bristol Aeroplane Co Ltd, English Electric Aviation Ltd, builders of the P1 Lightning, Hunting Aircraft Ltd and Vickers-Armstrong (Aircraft) Ltd, builders of the VC10).

The BAC 223 study had followed a proposal for a larger version – the Bristol Type 198 which had been considered too ambitious to gain Ministry approval.

The Type 198 design had been originally submitted as one of the feasibility studies which had followed the recommendations of the STAC. With transatlantic range at a cruise speed of Mach 2.2, it was to have had six Olympus engines in a bank on top of the wing under the fin. The projected all up weight was to be 385,000 lb, with a passenger load of 132. Concorde turned out to be only four per cent heavier with a similar load carrying ability and four Olympus engines of increased thrust instead of the original six.

The BAC 223 on the other hand, although still with transatlantic range, had a proposed weight of 270,000 lb and was to be powered by four under-wing mounted Olympus engines. This question of size as well as range was already causing much controversy. A great deal of unnecessary expense was incurred building tools and jigs for designs that were not produced.

Duncan Sandys, perceiving the political and economic advantages of collaboration between France and Britain, had encouraged Sir George Edwards, Chairman of the new BAC, to explore the possibilities of co-operation with his French opposite number, Georges Hereil of Sud Aviation. At first, there did not appear to much of a basis for co-operation due to the differing range philosophies. So discussions centred around collaboration on a common engine, on systems, electrics and hydraulics.

To achieve better coordination, the French Minister of Transport and Britain's Minister of Aviation met in September 1961. This resulted in a firm directive to the participating firms to resolve their differences. But collaboration proved more difficult for the airframe manufacturers, whose ideas on range were becoming more entrenched, than for the engine manufacturers. There was only one engine that could sensibly be used for both the medium and long haul SST: the Bristol-Siddeley Olympus.

Bristol Aero-engines had persevered privately with the Olympus in spite of Government policy which had decreed, in 1957, that there would be just the one large engine programme, centred on the Rolls-Royce Conway engine. Had it not been for the wisdom and foresight of Sir Reginald Verdon-Smith, Chairman of the Bristol Aeroplane Company, there would have been no engine immediately available and suitable for an SST.

There followed more meetings between

the respective ministers to encourage collaboration. There was little result at first, other than the making of a few conciliatory gestures – the building of the tail section of the Super VC10 was subcontracted out to a Sud Aviation subsidiary.

Then in 1962 de Gaulle came to power in France. General Andre Puget replaced Georges Hereil, while in Britain Julian Amery became the Minister of Aviation. These changes propelled the two countries into an agreement with one another. De Gaulle saw this as a way of improving the French Aircraft Industry while Puget, unlike Hereil, was on the same wavelength as George Edwards; Amery was to seal this concord with an unbreakable treaty.

Just before the signing of the treaty the Americans became perturbed by the progess being made in the field of SSTs in Europe. Accordingly Eugene Black, ex-Chairman of the World Bank and a

The Mirage III. The French pursued the delta planform after the British success with the FD2. The Mirage has been a great success for the French aircraft industry

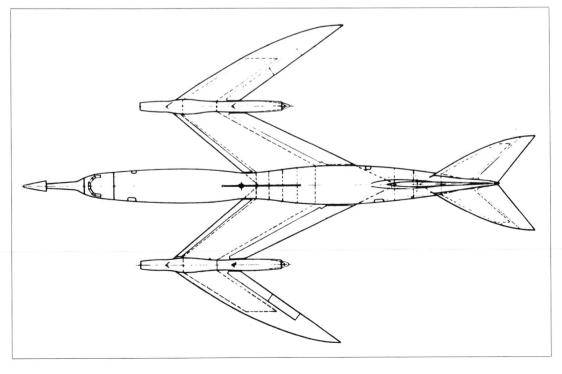

The medium range M-winged Mach 1.2 proposal from Armstrong Whitworth. The cone at the nose would have kept the nose shock wave clear of the wings. Area ruling, apparent where the fuselage is waisted, was intended to keep the drag down. Concorde was not quite long enough to have required area ruling

The Rolls-Royce/SNECMA Olympus 593–610 engine, powerplant for Concorde. Between 50,000 and 60,000 ft at Mach 2 it is the world's most efficient aero engine, with more than 40 per cent thermal efficiency. With re-heat on take-off it delivers over 38,000 lb of thrust, during the supersonic cruise around 10,000 lb

Concorde's family tree. The Super Caravelle and BAC 223 were only design studies. The Type 221 was a modification of the FD2

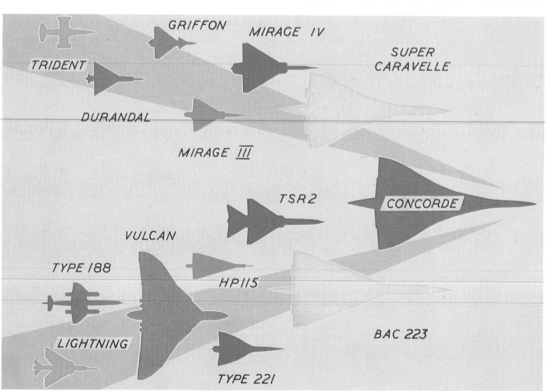

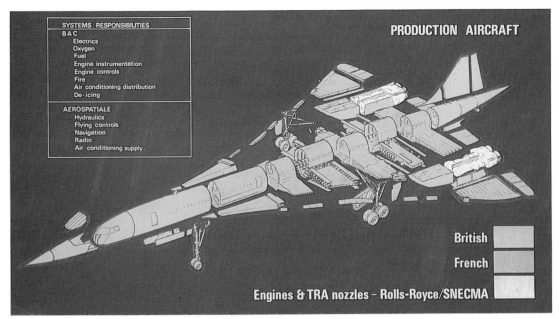

The distribution of responsibilities for the manufacture of Concorde. Broadly the breakdown between France and Britain was 60:40 for the airframe and 40:60 for the engine

prominent and influential individual in the US corridors of power, attempted to dissuade Julian Amery from continuing with his plans. According to Geoffrey Knight (one time director of BAC) in his book *Concorde the Inside Story* this merely had the effect of encouraging Amery to go ahead. The Americans were afraid that Britain's gamble was going to pay off. It turned out that Eugene Black was about to become Chairman of a high-powered committee set up to study the possibility of the United States building an SST.

On 29 November 1962 an agreement between the governments of France and Britain was signed and registered at the Hague. The agreement comprised seven articles. It included clauses about each country having equal responsibility for the project, bearing equal shares of the cost, and sharing equally the proceeds of sales. Two aircraft – a long-range and a medium-range one – were envisaged. Every effort was to be made to carry out this programme with equal attention to both the medium and long-range versions. There were to be two integrated organisations taken from British and French firms – BAC and Sud Aviation for the airframe, Bristol Siddeley and SNECMA for the engine – which were to make detailed proposals for carrying out the programme. There was no break clause. The agreement was signed by Julian Amery and Peter Thomas (Parliamentary Under-Secretary of State, Foreign Office) for the United Kingdom and G de Courcel, French Ambassador in Britain, for France.

It was the first time in history that such a collaborative organisation had been set up.

The bureaucratic machinery that was to control the project ensured three things. First that every decision was minutely and critically examined by both partners. Secondly, as a result of the first, a superior aircraft was to evolve. Thirdly, the process would take longer and cost more than if it had been organised individually or with one country having design leadership.

The first flight of the prototype was expected during the second half of 1966, while the first production aircraft was due at the end of 1968, with a Certificate of Airworthiness (C of A) being granted at the end of 1969. In the event, the first prototype flew in March 1969, and the C of A was granted in late 1975.

The development costs of the project in 1962 were put at between £150m and £170m. The division of responsibility was to be 60:40 between France and Britain on the airframe and 40:60 on the engine. For various reasons connected with inflation, devaluation of the pound, the reworking of the design in 1964 for just the long haul version and the longer time it took to complete, the project eventually cost, as we shall see, rather more!

Britain was not yet a member of the Common Market. As one commentator put it 'Concorde was conceived before the two contracting partners were joined in wedlock.' In spite of the agreement, membership of the EEC by Britain was put off a further nine years. So even this act of European unity, in the face of American aviation technology, was not enough; de Gaulle was still suspicious of Britain's special relationship with the United States.

Taking Shape

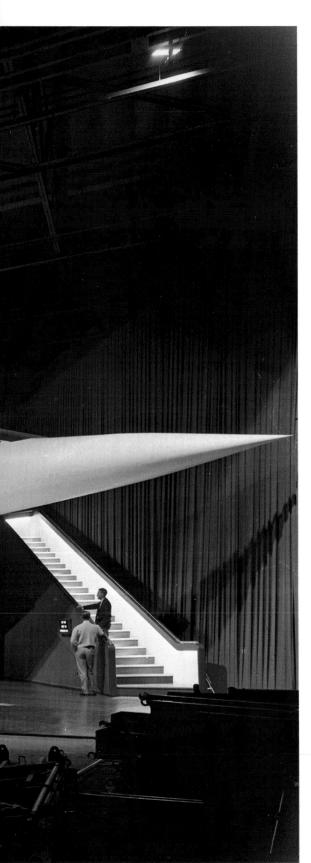

An SST has to operate in an extraordinarily hostile environment. At Mach 2 it experiences a freezing wind of such force that the fuselage is heated to the boiling point of water, shock waves tear at every angle on its airframe, and all this occurs at an altitude where the atmospheric pressure is a tenth of its value at sea level. Only military aircraft flown by pilots, equipped with sophisticated oxygen supplies and wearing pressure suits, had ventured to these extremes and then usually only for minutes at a time. The SST was designed to carry ordinary airline passengers in complete comfort and safety for hours at a stretch. Could the fusion of British and French philosophies possibly produce such a craft?

Judging from the expected timescale of the project there was confidence that success would come quickly. The physics of obtaining lift throughout the speed range was understood. The loss in aerodynamic efficiency at speeds above Mach 1 would be more than compensated by the improvement in the efficiency of the intake and engine combination achievable at Mach 2. A certain amount of ingenuity would be called for in some areas – notably in the engine air intake, air conditioning and fuel systems. Novel techniques, like the redistribution of the fuel in flight to maintain the balance of the aircraft, would have to be developed.

The aircraft also would need to behave in a way that pilots had been trained to expect. A slender delta-winged aircraft with no horizontal tail surfaces behaves differently from a swept-winged aircraft with a tail. It is less naturally stable in speed – a conventional aircraft is designed so that a speed increase over the tail surface causes an extra downforce on the tail. This pitches the aircraft into a climb which, without a thrust increase, restores the speed. Also its ratio of pitch to roll is different from a conventional aircraft because of its length and small wingspan. Rather than rely on excessive training time to teach pilots new techniques it would be safer to fit the aircraft with computers to give it the feel of a conventional aircraft.

The design was revolutionary. In spite of the very best endeavours of the designers there was no way of predicting the

The full scale wooden mock-up of Concorde at Filton, England. This mock-up was used to check emergency evacuation systems as well as being an example of the appearance of the finished product for prospective purchasers

The Convair B-58 Hustler bomber. An engine failure at supersonic speeds, on this delta aircraft, was barely survivable

An Avro Vulcan with five Olympus engines. The centre one – the Olympus 593 – is shown here undergoing icing trials. Water droplets, simulating flight in cloud, were released ahead of the intake from the device beneath the nose. An unchecked build up of ice within the intake and over the first compression stages of the engine would radically affect performance. Heat applied either electrically or from hot air on vulnerable surfaces overcomes the problem

interaction of *all* the systems before the first flight of the prototypes. There might be some totally unforeseen side effect which could take years to iron out, like some quirk in the airflow affecting just one engine, necessitating a control law peculiar to that engine alone. Indeed such a problem did arise, but mercifully a simple solution was found.

Having designed a practical aircraft, it would be worthless unless it were safe.

Making the structure safe, yet light, would stretch the powers of the designers. Having built the structure it would have to be tested to limits beyond those that could be explored in flight. To achieve that full scale versions of the airframe would have to be dedicated to ground-testing. All the stresses and strains of high altitude flight would be applied to them, including the repeated heating and cooling of the airframe, experienced on each supersonic flight to at least one of them.

Very high altitude flight is advantageous to an SST since it can fly at a far lower indicated airspeed for a given true airspeed (see page 11). At 60,000 ft travelling at Mach 2, or 1,150 knots true airspeed, Concorde only 'feels' 435 knots of airspeed. Fighter aircraft have to be built with sufficient strength to withstand turbulent air at indicated airspeeds in excess of 700 knots. Such a speed, apart from being quite unnecessary for an SST, would call for a stronger and therefore heavier structure. With the very small margin available of payload weight to total weight, the SST could not be allowed to have the luxury of a high indicated airspeed limit. The indicated airspeed limit on Concorde varies with altitude, reaching a maximum of 530 knots

A full sized rig was made to check the working of Concorde's fuel system. Apart from supplying the engines, the fuel is used to move the centre of gravity rearwards during acceleration and forwards prior to landing as well as being a medium for cooling the air in the air conditioning system and cooling the engine oil

at 43,000 ft. A typical limit for a subsonic passenger jet is 350 knots (see page 122).

Off-setting the advantage of flying high is the disadvantage that the fuselage has to be made strong enough to withstand high differential pressures. To give a cabin altitude of 6,000 ft when the aircraft is at 60,000 ft requires a differential pressure approaching 11 lb per square inch (psi). Hitherto the limit for subsonic jets had been about 8 lb psi which gave them a cabin altitude of over 7,000 ft at an aircraft altitude of 37,000 ft.

Large aircraft require a multitude of systems: electrics, hydraulics, navigation, undercarriage and flying controls to name but a few. Systems fundamental to the safety of the aircraft must have back up systems. Some systems on Concorde were to have additional back up systems. For instance, Concorde is fitted with four methods of lowering the undercarriage: two of them from different hydraulic sources; one by letting it down by its own weight; and a fourth by use of compressed air.

Before passengers could be carried every conceivable combination of failures and consequent recourse to back up systems

There are four undercarriage legs on Concorde, here seen at half travel. The length of the main gear legs is governed by having to keep the rear of the engines clear of the ground at the high aircraft pitch angles associated with take-off and landing. The tail gear is there as a precaution against this eventuality. The camber on the wing (roughly the amount that the leading and trailing edges are bent downwards), can be seen from this picture. It helps to minimise the rearward movement of the centre of lift with increasing Mach number, thus the requirement to move the centre of gravity so far rearward is also minimised

had to be explored. Might the warning of a failure of one system cause the pilots to take inappropriate action? Just prior to Concorde entering service it was discovered that the loss of some of the hydraulic pressure to the flying controls during the early stages of the take-off run resulted in an instruction to the pilots to abandon the take-off. This required the application of the wheel brakes, themselves requiring hydraulic pressure supplied from the source whose failure caused the take-off to be abandoned. Although hydraulic pressure to the brakes could be restored in seconds, that would be too late for an aircraft travelling at 270 ft per second: the aircraft would overrun. So an instantaneous and automatic change-over from one hydraulic supply to another had to be the solution.

Safety at the level of system failures was one thing, but would the SST be able to survive a potentially more catastrophic incident? Would it be controllable during conditions following the simultaneous failure of two engines on one side? The answer had to be 'yes'. But when the British and French prepared to join forces in 1961, experience of such incidents had not been good.

The world's first big supersonic jet was the four-engined, delta-winged American Convair B58 Hustler. It was not capable of surviving a single engine failure at Mach 2, let alone two on the same side. Even flight at other speeds was risky – a B58 crashed during a display at the 1961 Paris Airshow. Deaths of B58 crew were common occurrences in spite of their being housed in escape capsules. It would be small comfort for a Concorde passenger to think that the pilot and his crew were similarly protected while he was not!

No country had yet been called upon to award a Certificate of Airworthiness for the transport of the fare-paying public in an SST. New rules had to be introduced. Every detail of the new aircraft would suffer the expert scrutiny of the civil aviation authorities of Britain, France and, as a prospective purchaser, the United States.

There are conflicting requirements on any aircraft. On an SST such conflict is extreme: too strong and it would be too heavy; too efficient at one speed, it might be unflyable at another; highly efficient engines at Mach 2 might be noisy on take-off. Compromise and ingenuity would find solutions, but the margins were narrow. The payload to maximum take-off weight on the long range

The Concorde production line at Toulouse, France, the other line was at Filton, England. It is doubtful that any future collaborative project on the scale of Concorde would have duplicate production lines

Concorde 002 GBSST

Concorde 01 – the first pre production aircraft inside the 'Brabazon' hangar at Filton, Britain. Note the shorter tail cone found on this and the two prototype Concordes, and the original secondary nozzle system visible here on number three engine. On production aircraft this was replaced by variable 'buckets'

airliners of the 1960s was 10 per cent; the
Boeing 747s of the 1970s give 20 per cent.
The SST would be lucky to achieve 5 per
cent over a 3,500 nm range. A small error in
performance would remove the ability to
carry any payload between London and
New York (see page 118).

The small predicted payload to weight
ratio did not daunt the supporters of the
SST. The difference would be restored by
the greater number of Atlantic crossings
achievable by one aircraft. The price of fuel
was expected to remain constant, even fall a
little! The sonic boom, however, did cause
concern.

An aircraft travelling at speeds above
Mach 1.15, depending on atmospheric
conditions, causes a double boom to be
audible on the surface. Should this preclude
supersonic flight over populated land, the
medium-range SST espoused by the French
would be a non-seller, as there are too few
viable medium range routes which fly over
the sea (see sonic boom propogation
photograph, page 58).

In 1966 the designers hoped that two very
similar SSTs would be built. The medium-
range version would have space for more
passengers and less fuel whilst the long-
range version would reverse the mix. They
discovered, however, that each design
compromised the other. Coupled with
thoughts about the sonic boom, this finally
killed off the medium-range SST.

Nevertheless the two prototype Con-

cordes 001 and 002, whose building had
commenced in April 1965, could not be
described as long-range SSTs. The same
applied to the two pre-production Concordes – 01 and 02. The final production
version of Concorde (serial numbers from
201 to 216) was not only a long range SST
but also came very close to Archibald
Russell's original specification – the Bristol
Type 198. Designing, tooling and building of
three different versions of Concorde added
very greatly to the cost and the time spent on
the project. On top of this problem, the
whole project had duplicate headquarters,
at Filton and Toulouse, mainly for political
reasons. With hindsight it is absolutely
remarkable that such a fine aircraft as
Concorde could have had such a complicated beginning.

No less troublesome to the project were
the various changes of government on the
British side. No soon as one government
takes over, its predecessor's activities come
up for scrutiny. The Labour Government
which took over from the Conservatives in
1964 was a case in point. It was only the
agreement between France and Britain
jointly to build an SST – an agreement that
had been registered at The Hague – which
prevented cancellation of the project.

Pressure had also been mounting from
America for Britain to abandon various
aviation projects – among them the TSR2
supersonic military aircraft. Why should the
United States lend money to Britain only to

GAXDN (Concorde 01) landing at Farnborough

fund aircraft projects which would compete with the American aviation industry? According to Julian Amery, the British minister who had concluded the agreement with France, the Americans had insisted that Concorde should be stopped. George Brown, the Minister of Economic Affairs of the new 1964 Labour Government denied that this was so. Following publication of Geoffrey Knight's book *Concorde the Inside Story* in 1976, Lord George Brown accused Mr Knight (in a letter to *The Times*, 7 May 1976) of getting 'almost every strand of his story wrong', although he admitted that he had not read the book. Nevertheless Geoffrey Knight later confirmed that there had indeed been US pressure against Concorde.

At industry level the story was different. From Boeing (the company chosen to build the US SST) came support for the European project. At first sight it might seem odd that a rival should support a rival, but this support was mutual. Each company felt that

if its rival was allowed to continue, then its own chances were bettered. This was borne out by the plethora of difficulties that faced Concorde as soon as the United States SST project was cancelled in 1971. Sadly much of that difficulty came from ill-informed political manoeuverers. Happily that lobby has become far better informed.

On 2 March 1969, the day before I joined BOAC, these difficulties lay in the future. On that day, André Turcat (director of Flight Test Aerospatiale) was to attempt to take Concorde 001 into the air for the first time from Toulouse. As an observer of the television coverage I can well remember the occasion. Bad weather had delayed the flight but at last Concorde 001 was lining up for take off. About 30 seconds worth of take-off run would prove whether the preceding seven years had been spent in vain; they were not, she flew. It was an amazing moment.

Only the low speed and low altitude range of the flight envelope (combination of speed

and altitude at which an aircraft is allowed to fly) were to be explored on this day. Did the indications of speed and altitude correspond to those of the chase aircraft? The undercarriage was not even raised. Take-off and flight proved to be possible, but could the slender delta be made to land?

Some 35 minutes later Concorde 001 was on final approach at Toulouse, and all looked well. On touchdown, two clouds of dust and smoke were whisked from the wheels into the vortices over each wing. Maskell and Kuckemann had been right: a separated airflow had given lift even to an aircraft as big as Concorde. Though fully aware that far better pictures would be immediately available I nevertheless photographed the event from the television screen to have, as it were, a personal record of Concorde's first landing.

Some minutes later surrounded by cameras and microphones André Turcat announced in French and English, 'The big bird flies'. Far greater men than one future

Concorde pilot could now turn their attentions to future demands, secure in the knowledge that the first hurdle had been safely surmounted.

Just over one month later the British-assembled prototype Concorde 002 took-off from Filton with Brian Trubshaw (Chief Test Pilot of BAC) at the controls. John Cochrane was the co-pilot and Brian Watts the Flight Engineer. As the flight deck is over 35 ft above the runway on main wheel touch-down, of key assistance in landing is the radio altimeter. Concorde has two radio altimeters, on this occasion both failed, so the landing at Fairford, Concorde's British test flight base (on account of its long runway), had to be done by eye.

Just under six years of testing and building were to elapse before Concorde's first commercial flight. During that time crises of all sorts presented themselves: environmental, political, technical and economic. Concorde's surviving of them all, ranks as a modern wonder of the world.

On the flight deck of Concorde 002 Brian Trubshaw (Chief Test Pilot BAC) and John Cochrane (BAC Test Pilot) – the pilots of the first test flight of 002, 9 April 1969. Note the large empty box at the centre of the instrument panel – space for a 'moving map display' which was later removed

First flight of 001 at
Toulouse, 2 March
1969

Below G-BSST, 5,500
hours of flight
testing, about four
times as many as for
a similarly sized
subsonic aircraft,
were necessary before
Concorde could enter

scheduled service

Opposite page
Concorde 002 about
to land at Fairford in
Britain at the end of
her maiden flight, 9
April 1969. Fairford
was considered more
suitable as a test
flying base on
account of its runway

being longer than the
one at Filton

Right Concorde's first
landing at Toulouse,
2 March 1969. This
shot, from a black
and white television
screen, clearly shows
the vortices etched by
the smoke from the
tyres on touchdown

49

The Other Supersonic Transports

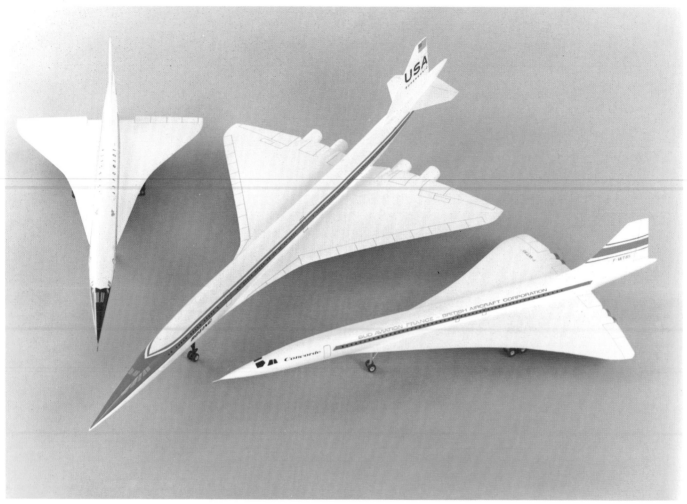

Of the three SSTs only Concorde became successful. The swing wing B2707-200 having proved too ambitious a project, Boeing resorted, in 1969, to the 2707-300 version (shown here as a model at centre). By 1971 the US government withdrew support even for this programme. (On the left is a model of the first version of the TU 144 and on the right a model of a prototype Concorde)

The flight deck of the Boeing 747 is situated above the first class passenger cabin. The decision to put it there was so that it would be easy to convert the airliner into a freighter. This could be done by fitting a cargo door in the nose and removing the seats. Boeing believed, during the design phase of the 747 in the mid 1960s, that supersonic transports would render their jumbos obsolete as passenger carriers, but not as freighters. They had good reason for their belief: the Concorde project had started in November 1962 and in June 1963 President Kennedy had announced that the US would develop an SST.

That announcement came after much lobbying of the President by the FAA (Federal Aviation Authority) administrator, Najeeb Halaby. He warned of dire consequences if the US were unable to build a challenger to Concorde, adding that the

President could conceivably find himself flying in a foreign aircraft. In the same way that Russian success had spurred on the US space programme, Concorde, especially after Pan Am announced its intention to buy six, catalysed the US reaction to SSTs. They would build one too.

To compensate for a late start the US SST had to be much larger and faster than Concorde. To this end a competition was planned, administered by the FAA, to look for the best airframe and the best engine. On 31 December 1966 it was decided that a Boeing design with swing wings (designated B2707-200) and powered by four General Electric engines was the aircraft to carry the US into the supersonic passenger age. The runner up in the competition had been the non-variable geometry Lockheed L-2000 – a proposal of similar shape to Concorde. Had the Lockheed version been

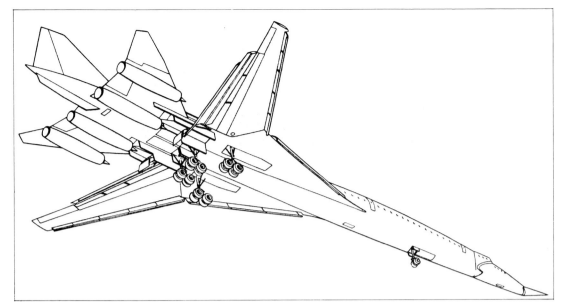

The Boeing 2707-200 of 1966. Note the presence of flaps and slats further complicating the engineering problems already associated with the swing wings

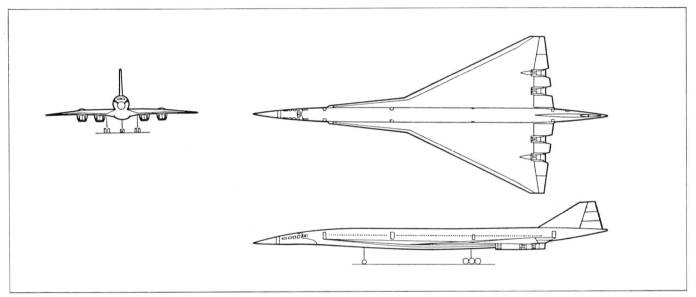

chosen, history might well have been very different. In April 1967 President Johnson gave the go-ahead for the next phase, a four year $1,600m prototype programme. Unlike previous US civil projects this one was to be financed on a 90:10 Government to industry ratio, changing to 75:25 for cost over-runs.

Half as long again as Concorde, the B2707-200 at 318 ft would have been the longest aircraft ever built. The design was intended to carry over 300 passengers at Mach 2.7 (about 1,800 mph) over 3,900 statute miles at altitudes up to 70,000 ft. Not only would its swing wings (fitted with conventional flaps and slats) give it a good take-off and landing performance, but they would give a higher aerodynamic efficiency at subsonic cruising speeds compared to a fixed delta design. Its maximum weight was to have been 675,000 lb (306,000 kg) almost one and three quarter times that of

Concorde. Each of the GE4 turbojet engines would have been capable of producing nearly 70,000 lb of thrust – not quite double that of Concorde. Due to the kinetic heating experienced at Mach 2.7, a titanium alloy would be required, such high temperatures (as hot as 260°C/500°F) being too great for aluminium alloys (see page 11).

By any definition it was an ambitious project and very quickly ran into difficulties. The hinge mechanism for the swing wings presented the greatest problem. For maximum effectiveness swing wings must have their pivots as close to the centreline of the aircraft as possible, since the greatest benefit of increased wing span can be so achieved. However, this interfered with the undercarriage and the positions of the engines. For it to be worth having swing wings their associated machinery must not be too heavy. By 1969 it appeared that their

History might have been different had Lockheed's proposal for an SST, the L2000, been chosen instead of Boeing's highly complex swing-wing one

51

Below *The double-jointed droop nose on this model of the Boeing 2707-200 displayed at the Boeing Museum of Flight during Concorde's visit to Seattle in November, 1984*

Cutaway model of the Boeing 2707-200 showing the right wing fully swept back. There was no left wing on the model

The right-hand wing of the Boeing 2707-200 in the fully swept position

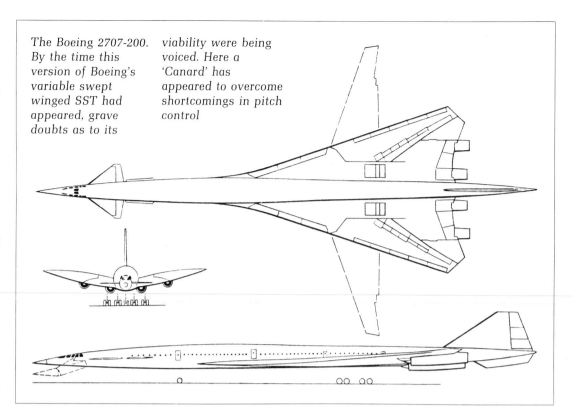

The Boeing 2707-200. By the time this version of Boeing's variable swept winged SST had appeared, grave doubts as to its viability were being voiced. Here a 'Canard' has appeared to overcome shortcomings in pitch control

Opposite top A good view of the underside of the later version of the TU 144. Compare the arrangement of the undercarriage, the intake boxes and the presence of a canard with the earlier version of TU 144

weight might be such that no payload could be carried.

So Boeing, unable to continue with the swing-wing project, submitted another design for FAA approval. The B2707-300 was somewhat similar to Concorde but it had a more marked double-delta wing and a tailplane. The same engines and as many of the original systems as possible were to be used. This time about 250 passengers were to be accommodated and the expected range was to be about 4,200 statute miles. But with a Mach 2.7 cruising speed, a titanium alloy, as yet not finally developed, would have been necessary. In comparison to Concorde's very simple arrangement of six elevon surfaces, the B2707-300 had a tailplane as well as control surfaces on the trailing edge of the wing. As with Concorde, the design of the B2707-300 became more difficult as it progressed. By 1970 political and environmental opinion was hardening against SSTs. Their future looked uncertain.

The environmentalists found allies among the US politicans critical of government expenditure on civil programmes. Had the same politicians withdrawn financial support from environmental programmes, then there would have been no joining of forces. As it was, both parties wanted the US SST to be cancelled. Notable among the politicians was Senator William Proxmire. Among the environmentalists were groups that delighted in such names as 'The Committee for Green Foothills' and 'Friends of the Wilderness'.

On 24 May 1971 they won their victory. The Senate and the House of Representatives both voted against further funds being made available for the US SST. For a sum of money about equal to that spent by Britain on Concorde, the US aerospace industry had nothing to show but tons of paperwork. Boeing's workforce at Seattle was drastically cut. Bleak though it was for Boeing, the Concorde protagonists knew

that their task was now harder. Without an American contender the full force of the environmentalists, flushed with victory, would be focused on them. Even the presence of the Soviet SST (the TU 144) would not count much in Concorde's favour. The technological mood in America, galvanised into such an intensive exploration of space by early Russian success had been assuaged by the moon landings. The TU 144 now appeared a relatively minor threat to prestige. The new creed among some in the US seemed to be: 'If you cannot beat them, then question the morality of their projects.'

In Russia nobody appeared to question the anachronism of an egalitarian state producing an aircraft suitable only for commissars. The TU 144 was not a copy of Concorde although superficially it looked very similar. It was supposed to be able to carry 121 passengers at Mach 2.35 (1,550 mph) over a distance of 4,000 statute miles – a performance which, on paper, was slightly

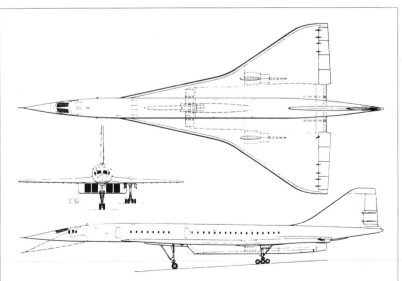

The first version of the TU 144 had the four separate engine intakes ducts contained within a single box. Note the absence of a canard. Although superficially similar to Concorde's wing in two dimensions, the TU 144's wing lacks the complex three dimensioned shaping found on Concorde

Model runways like this for the Concorde simulator at Filton have been superseded by computer generated images on later simulators. Note the TV camera flying over the surface which is in reality vertical. Concorde crews undergo simulator training and checking routines twice per year. About 60 hours of simulator flying is required during conversion to Concorde, the whole conversion process taking about six months

There still remains information on Novosibirsk in the computer of the Concorde simulator at Filton. Had the Tu 144 been a success, a trans-Russian route might have been possible. Note the runway lights visible through the windscreen when this picture was taken with the simulator 'pilotless' and 'frozen' on final approach

superior to that of Concorde. 'Concordski', as the TU 144 was dubbed, had a less complicated wing than her European rival. Instead of the ogival form with the curved leading edge joining the two angles of sweep-back, as on Concorde, the TU 144 was more distinctly a 'double delta'. The wing also exhibited less camber droop and twist than Concorde's. The four long engine intakes for the NK 144 turbofan engines were arranged in one box underneath the centreline but with dividing walls between them. The main gear was away from this box, retracting into a bay which protruded into blisters above and below the wing surface. There were no underfloor holds; baggage and freight were to be carried in panniers stowed between the two cabins and in a compartment to the rear over the engines.

The TU 144 however chalked up several 'firsts'. On 3 December 1968 she made her maiden flight, two months ahead of Concorde. In June 1969 Mach 1 was exceeded and in May 1969 Mach 2 was achieved. The respective dates for Concorde 001 (F-WTSS) were October 1969 and November 1970. However, there were problems with the Russian design as Sir George Edwards, Chairman on BAC, had pointed out to the Russians in 1967. The engines were in the wrong place, too close inboard; presumably they had been so positioned to make the aircraft easier to control in the event of engine failure. The engines were 'turbofans' and this would impair efficiency during supersonic cruise. The wing was not sufficiently sophisticated which would impair effectiveness and efficiency throughout the speed range.

At its appearance in the 1973 Paris Airshow, the TU 144 looked to have been radically redesigned. The pairs of engine intakes were now in two separate boxes, placing the engines further outboard, while the main undercarriage legs now retracted into a compartment within the engine intakes. A retractable 'canard' or foreplane appeared, placed above, and just to the rear of the flight deck. Extended, the canard would improve low speed flying characteristics by giving a lifting force to the front of the aircraft. This would now be countered by the elevons to the rear of the wing controlling the aircraft in pitch (and roll) going a few degrees down, thus giving 'flap' effect to the wing. Retracted, the canard would not interfere with the supersonic airflow. The Boeing 2707-200 (swing-wing)

design eventually included a canard too; but it was non-retractable and was there to assist control in pitch. To be fair, Concorde also appeared in progressively superior forms, but never with such a radical change as that exhibited by the TU 144.

Tragically the new version of the TU 144 crashed at the 1973 Paris Airshow. It appeared to be attempting to recover from a dive, but no really satisfactory explanation has been put forward for the disaster. On 26 December 1975 the TU 144, which apparently had not been modified greatly following the tragedy, entered service

between Moscow and Alma-Ata, capital of Kazakstan. It carried mail and freight over this 1,800 statute mile sector and flew at about Mach 2.05, between 52,500 and 59,000 ft for much of the distance.

By 1985, if not years before, the TU 144 was out of service. There were unconfirmed reports of another accident, but such events, unless they involve foreigners, are usually cloaked in Soviet secrecy. There is no evidence to believe that the TU 144 ever achieved its design range and payload. On the contrary, it almost certainly had to use the afterburners (reheat) during cruise, and

so it is unlikely that it had sufficient engine efficiency to fly transatlantic ranges.

This failure had one effect on Concorde. There had been plans for a trans-Soviet service by Concorde to Japan stopping at Moscow and Novosibirsk. With no TU 144 to take up reciprocal rights, the Soviet authorities were unlikely to approve a scheduled Concorde route over Russia. A last memorial to this plan remains. In the computer for the Concorde flight simulator at Filton there exists information about Novosibirsk, available should BA crews ever have needed training for this airfield.

A Stormy Beginning

Early in the 20th century, self-propelled road-going vehicles in England had to be preceded by a man with a red flag. The rule did not reflect the politics of the day but was made because of the vehicles' speed. Whether those who criticized Concorde were motivated by this type of conservatism will never be known; nevertheless there was vociferous opposition against SST's in general and Concorde in particular. The criticism came from all quarters: journalists (on both sides of the Atlantic), an English bishop, politicians (mainly from America), and many other individuals. Their arguments were based on economic and environmental grounds and were often completed with the question: 'What's the use of people travelling so fast in any case?'

When the American SST was cancelled in 1971, a US Senator declared that if the project was worth financing then Wall Street, not the Government, should do it. By 1976 Concorde had absorbed in development costs alone about £500m from Britain and the same amount from France – rather less it was said, than that spent on the abandoned US SST. Concorde certainly had rather an expensive aura to it. Nevertheless it would be churlish for any American politician to maintain that the successful US civil transports, like the series of Boeing and Douglas passenger jets, had not benefited financially from the military contracts that paved the way for their development. But with no military counterpart, the US SST as well as Concorde had to be developed and paid for almost from scratch.

Concorde's development bill had suffered in three ways: firstly from inflation; secondly from the costs associated with having two equal partners (according to one source this accounted for as much as 30 per cent of the bill); and thirdly from having produced three substantially different versions of the aircraft – the two prototypes, the two pre-production aircraft and finally the production series. It was easy to see the critics point of view: that vast amounts of money had been spent so that the 'idle' rich could save a few hours travelling time. But Concorde was never designed for the idle. On the contrary it was designed for busy people who add to the wealth of their businesses and the economies of the free world. Given that each generation benefits from the preceding one, would every Concorde critic, had he been in a position to do so, have protested at the development of the car in the days when it was exclusively used by a minute proportion of the population.

Even as late as 1976 critics were pressing

for Concorde to be abandoned on economic grounds. But by then the development phase was virtually over, so cancellation would have ensured that all the money spent and experience acquired would have been largely in vain. Those who suggested that Concorde's development money should really have been allocated to other more 'worthy' causes were being over optimistic. It is unlikely that the small amount that would have been made available by cancellation in 1963 (about £40m) would, as a matter of policy, have been chanelled elsewhere.

A more serious criticism is that Concorde prevented investment in other aviation projects. Would the BAC 3-11 (a wide bodied, twin engined, medium range airliner) have survived in the early 1970's? Or would Britain have remained a full member of the European Airbus consortium? As for the BAC 3-11, the answer is probably yes, bearing in mind that Governments often withdraw their support from aviation projects; but without the agreement to build Concorde, the Airbus Consortium would not have come into being when it did, so the second question is hypothetical.

Alongside their economic arguments, critics added environmental ones. One criticism was that the ozone layer might be dispersed and the ultra-violet light shield removed thus causing skin cancer to become endemic. Others mentioned physical damage caused by sonic booms, passengers suffering excess doses of radiation from solar flares, pollution of the atmosphere with poisonous emission and finally Con-

corde being too noisy on or near the ground.

Concorde's manufacturers patiently answered all these questions. On the first point, ozone is present in the stratosphere, which is the layer of atmosphere above the tropopause. Between the tropopause (average altitude 37,000 ft) and the surface of the earth, is the troposphere, which is that part of the atmosphere where weather occurs. (See Appendices, page 122.) Concorde's engines emit nitric oxide which reacts with ozone to form nitrogen dioxide. Without 'cleansing' from the trophosphere, the stratosphere would lose ozone and gain nitrogen dioxide. It was feared that without absorption by the ozone the extra ultra-violet light from the sun could cause a higher incidence of skin cancer. However, an American investigation, called the Climatic Impact Assessment Program (CIAP), refuted the current theory that the 30 SST's then scheduled to enter service would have any detectable effect on the stratosphere. Furthermore natural variations in the quantity of ozone would make the assessment of the impact of even 125 Concordes flying four hours per day above 50,000 ft impossible to discern.

On the sonic-boom problem, the British desire to build only a long-range SST was based on the belief that sonic booms would usually be intolerable over populated land, but would be allowable on long-range routes which were over oceans, desert or tundra. On some others a small detour adding maybe 100 to 200 miles (5 to 10 minutes flying time) could allow continuous supersonic operation through avoidance of

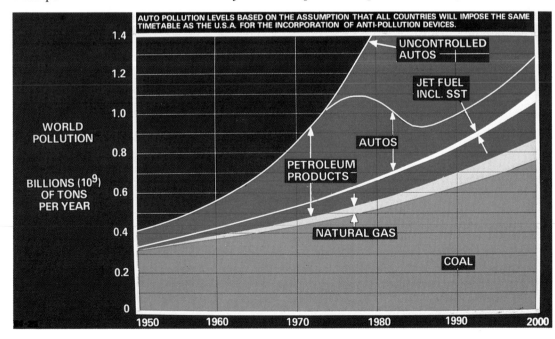

A pollution chart published in 1976 showing the very small amounts of pollution attributable to jet engines, let alone SSTs

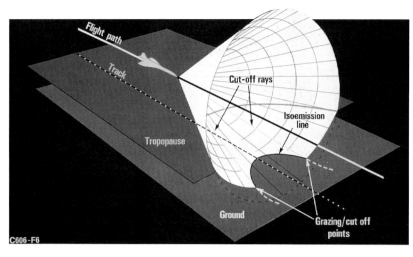

The direction of the 'ray' path of the shock wave is at right angles to the line of the wave. As the shock waves descend into the warmer air near the earth's surface their path bends concave to the sky. Thus shock waves generated by aircraft at low supersonic Mach numbers are not heard on the surface, having been refracted upwards, in a way analogous to a mirage

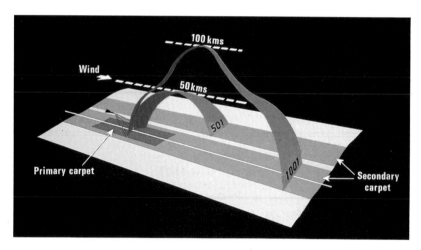

A portion of the upgoing wave can be refracted back to the surface forming a secondary boom. The guns of the western front in France, during the First World War, were heard faintly in certain places in England, on still evenings, further from them, than in others, closer to them, due to this effect. During the winter when the upper westerly winds are stronger, eastbound Concordes decelerate through Mach 1 further from a 'boom sensitive' coast to minimise this effect

Under some conditions the shock wave can bounce, as shown here. The amount of energy returning to earth from these effects is tiny. Loose windows can sometimes be rattled by them, as by a gust of wind. The reflected and refracted boom is usually inaudible unless the ambient noise is virtually zero

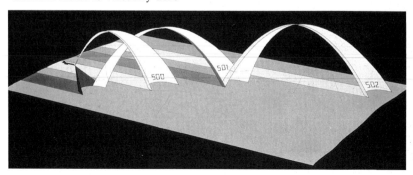

'boom sensitive' land. Where there was no way round, the higher subsonic cruising speed of an SST would give it a small edge, about 100 mph, over the majority of subsonic aircraft. Most Concorde routes do include a small proportion of flight at Mach 0.95.

On the question of solar flares, Concorde is fitted with a radiation meter. The usual dosage rate of cosmic radiation over the latitudes between London and New York at 55,000 ft is around 1 millirem per hour (about twice that found at 35,000 ft). Solar flares could cause the dosage rate to exceed 50 millirem per hour. In every case so far, the presence of radiation from a solar flare has been forecast since the flare can be seen about a day before the associated radiation reaches the earth. If radiation were encountered Concorde would descend to an altitude where, shielded by more atmosphere above, the radiation rate is lower. A survey used in 1976 showed that such evasive action would have had to have taken place five times during the previous 39 years. No radiation warnings from space have been received on Concorde during the first 10 years of commercial operation. Although the dosage rate on a subsonic aircraft is half as much, the occupants experience the effect for twice as long, thus receiving a similar quantity to that received by a Concorde passenger. Furthermore subsonic flights over the poles, where the radiation is higher, expose the aircraft's passengers to more radiation.

Placing this all in context, an individual's dose of radiation from all sources, including cosmic rays, X-rays, television sets and atmospheric nuclear tests accumulates to about 100–150 millirem per year, and one transatlantic crossing in a subsonic or supersonic transport adds 3 millirem to that total. There are greater dangers to be found from crossing the road than from this. Suggestions that Concorde should only be staffed by stewardesses beyond child bearing age, just turned out to be stories designed to attract popular press headlines.

As far as the pollution of the atmosphere is concerned only hydrogen-fuelled engines are completely 'clean' – that is if the water vapour they emit is ignored. Fossil-fuelled engines also emit water vapour. Often the critics could not make up their minds whether the presence of extra water vapour would 'cut off the sun's rays from the ground and bring on a new ice age', or 'give rise to a "hot house" effect and overheat the

earth'. In practice the earth's weather systems are infinitely more responsible for the distribution of water vapour than aircraft can ever be. As for other pollutants, cars are nearly ten times worse per seat mile than Concorde, and there are many cars.

Of the most serious concern to the critics was the noise that they believed Concorde would cause at airports. For efficiency at supersonic speeds SSTs then had to be fitted with engines which have a high velocity jet efflux. The shearing effect of this efflux with the static air to the rear of an aircraft causes the major part of the noise. Consistent with retaining an efficient engine, Concorde's manufacturers had gone to enormous lengths to reduce engine noise. They had concentrated on two areas. One was to break down the sharp boundary between the moving and static air and the other was to try and increase the quantity of air flowing through the engine so that it would give the same thrust with a lower exhaust velocity.

The first line of attack saw the development of a device called 'spades'. These were designed to break up the efflux by protruding rectangular metal plates into the jet pipe to splay out the jet efflux during take-off, to be retracted when engine silencing was not required. The 'spades' appeared quite promising in miniature, but failed to be sufficiently effective on the full-scale engine, and were abandoned. Another device called 'buckets' was more successful. Consisting of a pair of doors rather like eyelids, they are set to the rear of the jet pipe of each engine, being visible from the outside of the aircraft. During flight at low speed they mix the static and engine exhaust air thus breaking up the noisy boundary. On landing they are used as thrust reversers by closing off the jet pipe and deflecting the efflux forward; in supersonic flight they form a divergent exit nozzle (see photograph on page 22).

The second line of attack on the noise front involved computer control of the relative speeds of two engine shafts allowing the engine to 'change gear'. This happens after Concorde takes-off and allows a greater mass of air into the engine, thus causing the velocity of the jet efflux to be reduced without the loss of thrust. Such a process can only be applied after Concorde has sufficient forward speed for the intakes to swallow enough air; insufficient air could lead to a surge (backfire).

Whatever the manufacturers achieved in

G-BSST taking off. Later marks of the Olympus engine were to have a modified combustion chamber which virtually eliminated these smoky emissions and some of the criticism. On later versions of the intake, the auxiliary inlet doors were of the 'blow-in type, not the scoop type as shown here

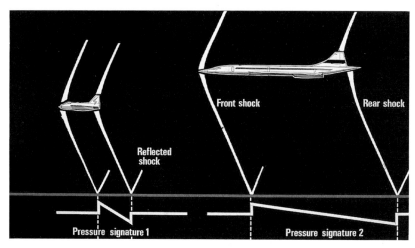

The pressure signatures from supersonic aircraft of different lengths. Note this diagram does not show the refraction of the shock waves due to increasing temperature and changing winds as they approach the earth's surface

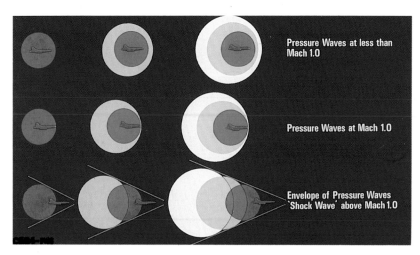

the way of noise reduction, the crews having reduced to minimum thrust consistent with climbing, to comply with noise abatement procedures had to eke out every last ounce of the aircraft's performance. However, such procedures had not been finally and accurately formulated for use during the route proving flights flown by Concorde during the summer of 1975. Concorde was thus rather noisier than she should have been, with the result that the American anti-Concorde lobby found some rather willing allies in Britain.

The worst aspect of the anti-Concorde campaign was the way in which the critics were quite happy to see Concorde written off before being allowed into New York without a fair noise trial. There was much discussion in the media about this but eventually, when services began, the combination of the relatively light take-off weights (less fuel is required on a New York to London sector than vice versa) and the meticulous application of the noise abatement procedures kept Concorde's noise well within limits. The protestors melted away. Since then Concorde has made many firm friends with the people in New York.

Nevertheless a second generation SST will have to be quieter than Concorde. Several fully laden Concorde departures per day can be tolerated by most people but one every ten minutes from the more land locked airfields could be problematic.

The noise monitoring posts at Kennedy. The two most desirable runways for Concorde on take-off are 31L and 22R. By turning away from the noise sensitive areas after take-off, most of the noise impact of Concorde at Kennedy was avoided. Runways 4L, 4R and 13L are never used by Concorde at transatlantic take-off weights

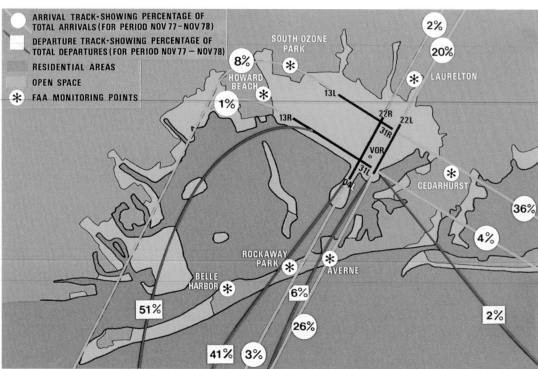

The inaugural take-off to Bahrain from runway 28L at Heathrow, 21 January 1976

Opposite
The build up of the shock waves. As the aircraft approaches the speed of sound, the molecules of air progressively have less 'warning' of the approach of the aircraft. Above Mach 1 a shock wave forms, tangential to the spheres of disturbance. Some Concorde critics appeared to think that Concorde formed a shock wave at any speed. Under normal conditions, due to its refraction in the warmer atmosphere beneath the aircraft, the shock wave from Concorde only reaches the ground when Concorde exceeds Mach 1.15. The shock wave first reaches the ground about 50 miles after the 'acceleration point'

In January 1976 the final battle for entry to New York still lay in the future. British Airways and Air France were patiently putting the finishing touches to a plan for a joint take-off into the supersonic era; the British with a Concorde from Heathrow and the French with a Concorde from Charles de Gaulle.

On 21 January 1976 I stood with my wife, camera at the ready at the take-off end of runway 28 left at London's Heathrow airport. Around us were crowds of people, some were wearing heavy looking 'service' earphones connected to electronic devices wired up to microphones on poles. Concorde would not start her commercial supersonic service unrecorded! We listened to a local radio broadcast. At 11.40 precisely the commentator announced that Concorde had begun to roll. Next came the distinctive sound of the four reheated Olympus engines. Then Concorde GBOAA came in view, climbing out over the approach lights

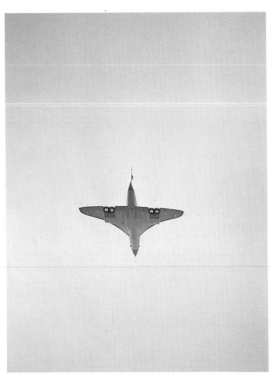

*Airlife, 1984

of the reciprocal runway, with the under-carriage retracting. Commercial supersonic services had begun.

As the British Concorde, under the command of Captain Norman Todd, with Captian Brian Calvert as second-in-command and senior Engineer Officer John Lidiard reached her subsonic cruising altitude over the English Channel, the crew heard that the Air France Concorde F-BVFA had had an equally successful departure. The odds, people had said, were heavily against achieving a simultaneous take-off, but as so often in the past Concorde had proved the pessimists wrong.

Concorde F-BVFA flew to Rio de Janeiro via Dakar; G-BOAA flew to Bahrain. Included amongst the guests on G-BOAA were Sir George Edwards (Chairman of BAC) and Sir Stanley Hooker. On arrival at Bahrain they were invited to a banquet at the New Palace by the Amir of Bahrain. Sir Stanley Hooker, in his book *Not Much of an Engineer*,* said: 'Eventually we entered the fabulous dining room, ritually washed our hands and took our places around the gigantic U-shaped table. I was next to the Minister of Foreign Trade, who spoke perfect English. We each had a waiter in full court uniform, each pair of guests being supervised by a steward . . . I was about to turn to the Minister and say "How far sighted and generous of your government to allow us to bring the Concorde here on its first scheduled flight" when he said to me "what a great honour you have done our country by bringing your magnificent Concorde here on its inaugural flight!" Considering the violent hullabaloo that was going on in New York, and that nobody else would allow us in, it was difficult to find the right answer!'

This publicity photograph, inset, was taken on Concorde G-BBDG (202) as can be seen from the instrumentation on the engineers' panel which was different from that ultimately fitted to the production Concordes

Manufacturers cut-away diagram of Concorde

Opposite page In contrast to her difficulties in 1976 and 1977 Concorde has become a welcome visitor to many US destinations. In November 1984 Concorde GBOAB visited Boeing Field at Seattle, Washington State. Mount Rainier can be seen in the background. For the visit the Boeing Museum of Flight displayed a model of the cancelled US SST project, the B2707-200; they also organised a supersonic flight by Concorde out over the Pacific and back for one hundred passengers to raise funds for the museum

Left to right *Senior Engineer Officer John Lidiard, Captain Norman Todd and Captain Brian Calvert – the crew of the inaugural service to Bahrain on 21 January 1976 on Concorde G-BOAA.*

The Turn of the Tide

During the early days of supersonic services to Bahrain in 1976, Concorde was hardly ever out of the headlines. 'US warned against ban on Concorde'; 'Court challenge on Concorde go-ahead'; 'Red light delays Concorde'; 'Boeing tries for rival to Concorde.' Under this headline from *The Times* (3 April 1976) Mr Lloyd Goodmanson, Boeing's design director said '... much of the official opposition to giving British Airways and Air France landing rights for Concorde was based on pure jealousy of their commercial lead rather than environmental considerations.'

Concorde had many vociferous friends and enemies. But for Concorde to succeed she needed landing rights in the United States, and at New York in particular.

Two production lines for Concorde had been set up at vast expense, one in Toulouse, France, and the other at Filton, in Britain.

Apart from the availability and skills of a work force, production lines require the necessary jigs and tools, but above all factory space. In 1974 the Governments of Britain and France had approved the building of 16 production Concordes. This was in spite of Pan American and TWA having decided in 1973 not to take up their options on buying Concorde. It was hoped that now Concorde had started services, these airlines might change their minds.

Iran Air and China Airlines had also shown an interest in Concorde, but they, in line with the rest of the world's airlines, were keeping very quiet on the subject. Production lines cannot remain open indefinitely while aircraft cannot go on being produced without prospective customers, and Concorde production facilities would have to make way for other work. By 1976 it was deemed that it was up to Air France and

Meeting at Dulles tower. Scheduled Concorde services to Washington's Dulles airport began on 24 May 1976

Opposite page A slender delta pivots around the slender CN tower. Concorde is a frequent visitor to the Toronto Airshow in Canada

British Airways to make a success of the new supersonic era. However, without permission to fly to the USA, this appeared almost impossible.

On 4 February 1976, after protracted wrangling, the US Secretary of Transportation, William T. Coleman, finally gave approval for British Airways and Air France to commence services for a 16 month trial period; one Concorde each per day to Washington and two each per day to New York. On 24 May 1976 Concorde services began to Dulles airport at Washington, owned by the Federal (US Government) authorities. In the words of Brian Calvert, Commander of that first flight: 'Planning started for what, it was decided, would be another spectacular – this time a joint arrival. We agreed that on this occasion the British Airways flight would land first – simultaneous landings were a little too much to expect.' The two Concordes performed perfectly, as they had done almost exactly four months earlier at the start of their commercial careers.

Landing Concorde at Dulles International airport Washington, was one thing, but permission to do so at Kennedy airport, New York, owned by the Port of New York Authority, was another. Coleman had implied that Federal pressure might be brought to bear on the Authority, but it became increasingly apparent that there would have to be a legal battle before Concorde could gain rights into New York.

Those rights were finally granted, and amidst threats of the greatest car-borne anti-SST demonstration, Concorde 201 (F-WTSB) arrived in New York on 19 October 1977. In command was Aerospatiale's Chief Test Pilot, Jean Franchi and on the flight deck with him were Captain Brian Walpole (BA Flight Technical

Manager) and Captain Pierre Dudal of Air France. The following day with Captain Walpole in command, Concorde took off from runway 31L (the left hand of the two north-westerly facing runways at New York). For the first time Concorde made the famous left hand climbing turn, started at 100 ft above the runway. That turn, which was regarded as cheating the noise meters by some critics, had been the subject of much practice, both at other airfields and in the Concorde simulators. The turn, the maintenance of the correct speeds, the cutting back of the thrust, the re-application, the cutting back and finally the re-application of thrust had been calculated precisely to correspond with Concorde's proximity to noise sensitive areas. The take-off was a success, the noise minimal. In one sense the protestors had won a great victory: Concorde had been made to be acceptably quiet and other airliners had better follow Concorde's example. On 22 November 1977 British Airways and Air France commenced supersonic services to New York.

Had there been no delay in starting the New York service, there might have been further orders for Concorde. But however 'well dressed' Concorde had appeared, no purchasers were forthcoming while she had 'nowhere to go.'

In December 1977 British Airways, in conjunction with Singapore Airlines (SIA), extended the London to Bahrain Concorde service to Singapore. During performance and hot weather trials in September 1974 the first 'production' Concorde (GBBDG), with Brian Trubshaw and Peter Baker (Assistant Chief test pilot BAC) at the controls, had flown supersonically over India. Supersonic overflying permission was now withdrawn so the Concorde route to Singapore had to go to the south of Sri Lanka adding some 200 nautical miles (10 minutes flying time). By December 1977 minor modifications and improved operating procedures had increased Concorde's range, so, what would have been unattainable in early 1976, was by then quite possible. However, after three return flights the Malaysian government withdrew flying rights over the Straits of Malacca. After more negotiations with the Malaysians the route reopened in January 1979 and was operated until November 1980. Concorde was flown to Singapore by BA crews with the cabin alternatively being staffed by BA and Singapore Airlines cabin crews.

World recession brought about a drop in

Concorde's load figures between London and Singapore. This, coupled with the financial arrangements between British Airways and Singapore Airlines, put a greater share of the burden of loss onto British Airways, finally caused the route to be abandoned. A particular Concorde had been earmarked for use on this route (G-BOAD), being painted in Singapore livery on the left hand side, and in BA colours on the right. This was the first and, by 1985, the only Concorde to have appeared in colours of an airline other than those of Air France or British Airways. Sadly, as the route closed down, the BA flight deck crews returned home from their postings in Singapore. With an excess of crews, some would leave and others be redeployed in the airline. Morale which was usually very high, took a temporary dip. G-BOAD was restored to BA livery.

Earlier that same year the agreement between Air France, British Airways and Braniff which enabled Concorde to continue through to Dallas, Texas from Washington (changing to an all American crew just for this sector), was wound up. The route lasted from January 1979 until June 1980. Braniff was, by 1985, the only American airline to have operated Concorde, albeit subsonically. They had hoped to gain experience with the aircraft for eventual supersonic services to South American destinations. In the meantime Concorde's high profile would have helped their marketing effort. But world recession and the deregulation of American internal airline routes had stretched Braniff's resources, so their Concorde operation experienced unacceptably low loads. On the Washington to Dallas sector the Concordes bore their home airlines' livery, the only noticeable external change being the dropping of the 'G' in the registration which in the case of the British Concorde had been changed from the usual British registration of a 'G' followed by four letters, to a 'G' followed by an 'N' two single digit numbers and the two final letters of the original British registration.

To give Concorde a boost during the time when services were declining, several Concorde crew members chartered the aircraft, giving people flights on Concorde at a fraction of the cost of a transatlantic fare. The first one to do so was a Concorde stewardess, Jeannette Hartley, who organised charters, at no little financial risk to herself. In 1981 my wife and I chartered Concorde to celebrate Britain winning the Schneider Trophy contest. The last contest was won in 1931 by an RAF team captained by Squadron Leader A. H. Orlebar*. In 1981 Concorde flew on two occasions, at 340 mph, almost exactly 1000 mph less than her cruising speed, around the final course which was situated between the Isle of Wight and Portsmouth (England). The speed of 340 mph was chosen since it had

Overleaf *G-BOAD* showing Singapore Airlines colours on the port (left) side, taking off from Heathrow for the nine hour journey to Singapore

*A cousin of the Author.

NEW YORK POST, THURSDAY, MAY 12, 1977

"Damn the court, DON'T LET IT LAND!!"

Opposite, below Concorde G-BOAA with the Anglo American registration G-N94AA during the period when Braniff operated Concordes between Washington Dulles and Dallas Fort Worth. Note the curves on the leading edge of the wing, necessary for the smooth transition from lift generated by vortices, roughly below 250 knots, to lift from a 'conventional' attached airflow, generated at the higher speeds

Concorde was chartered on 12 and 13 September, 1981, by the author to mark this event. Each of the passengers received a certificate like this one. The Captain on those occasions was John Eames, the author was First Officer and Senior Engineer Officer David Macdonald, the Flight Engineer

been the average speed of Flt. Lt. John Boothman's winning Supermarine S6B in 1931. Two Schneider trophy pilots flew on Concorde to celebrate the 50th Anniversary of the final victory: Air Commodore D'Arcy Greig (1929 team) and Group Captain Leonard Snaith (1931 team).

Other Concorde crew members followed suit.

On Concorde's financial side, a review in February 1979 of the ability of British Airways to make a profit with Concorde had concluded that it could not do so by ordinary commercial standards. Accordingly the Labour Government decided to write off the £160m of Public Dividend Capital (PDC) associated with BA's acquisition of its five Concordes. In November 1979 an Industry and Trade Select Committee, chaired by Sir Donald Kaberry MP, was convened. This was to investigate Concorde. Quoting from the report of their investigations (published in 1981): '... this [the writing off of £160m PDC] meant that the whole fleet, including the initial inventory of spares, was entered in the British Airways balance sheet as a fully depreciated asset – that is to say a gift from the taxpayer. For their part British Airways had to pay to the Government 80 per cent of future Concorde operating surpluses (the so called 80:20 agreement), though these were to be calculated after the offset of any operating deficits incurred after the review and also the amortised cost of any post-review expenditure.'

The BA partnership deal with Singapore Airlines (SIA) on the Singapore route negotiated by Gordon Davidson (Concorde Marketing Director, BA 1975–1979), appeared promising for BA, but it had dashed

Government hopes of SIA purchasing at least one of the remaining unsold Concordes – two in Britain and three in France. Later the best return for the Government appeared to come from placing the two unsold

SCHNEIDER TROPHY
50th Anniversary Flight by
British airways Concorde

1931   1981

British

Presented to

_____

who flew in Concorde to mark the event
on 13th September 1981

British Concordes with British airlines. When Gordon Davidson moved to British Caledonian, rumours started of BCal operating a supersonic service to Lagos, but this came to nothing. For a period BA operated one of the two surplus Concordes when one of its Concordes was undergoing modifications. Ultimately BA acquired the two remaining Concordes, making seven in all.

According to the Report, the UK had

spent about £900 million on Concorde by the end of 1980. Furthermore the Government was still having to finance the support given by the manufacturers to the project, expected to total £123 million for the five years beginning 1980/81.

During the commercial life of an aircraft, its manufacturers not only undertake to supply spare parts, but just as importantly to supply a 'support' service in the form of carrying out development work and monitoring performance, suggesting or insisting, where necessary, on improvements or modifications. Overseeing this process are the aviation authorities in whose countries the aircraft are built and registered – the CAA (Civil Aviation Authority) in Britain. These aviation authorities have the full backing of their country's law behind them. Such support is usually financed from profits from the sale of spare parts to the airlines.

In the case of Concorde, monitoring of the aircraft's performance was, in the early days of operation, a very expensive business. Not least of those expenses were the two test specimens – full-sized Concorde fuselages dedicated to being tested on the ground. Quite early in the programme the stress test specimen in France had been purposely tested to destruction, but the one at Farnborough, was still by 1980 costing several millions per year to run. This Concorde had been dedicated to being 'flight cycled', which included the heating and cooling process experienced on every supersonic sector. Profits through sales of spare parts would not raise anything like enough to pay for the Farnborough rig, nor enough to pay for the necessary, but diminishing, development work associated with Concorde. Accordingly, the four manufacturers – Aerospatiale, British Aerospace (successors to BAC), Rolls-Royce and SNECMA – were funded for their responsibilities to Concorde by their respective governments.

In October 1978 the jigs used to manufacture Concorde were removed from the Brabazon Hangers at Filton for storage at Wroughton, near Swindon in Wiltshire, against the possibility that there might be a demand for more Concordes. However, the French had, by December 1977, not only removed but disposed of their jigs; with their capability gone further production of Concordes would have been an extra expense. On 31 December 1980 it was announced that the production phase of Concorde had ended, but it was not until

The Stress Fatigue Specimen at CEAT (Centre d'Essais Aeronautique de Toulouse), one of the two complete Concorde airframes dedicated to structural tests. This specimen was not subjected to heating and cooling to simulate a supersonic flight cycle, as was the one at Farnborough

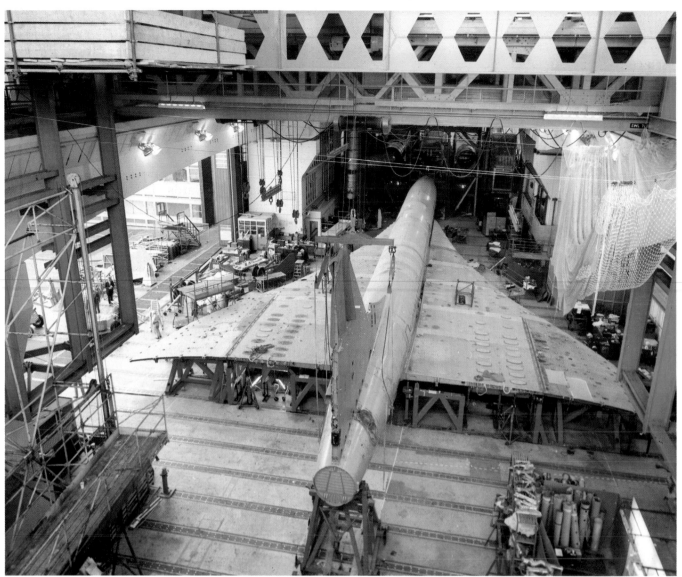

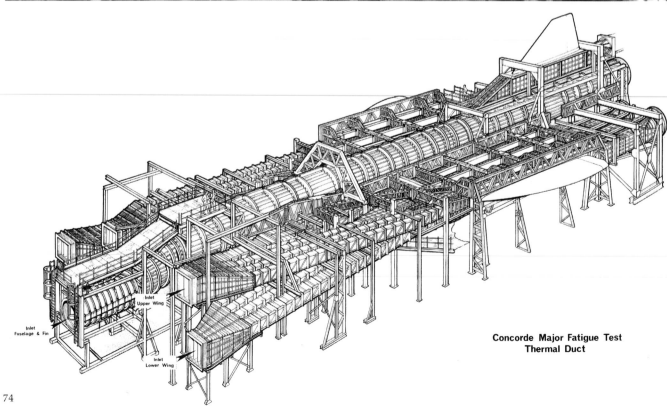

Inlet
Fuselage & Fin

Inlet
Upper Wing

Inlet
Lower Wing

**Concorde Major Fatigue Test
Thermal Duct**

October 1981 that disposal to scrap merchants of the stored British jigs began. About this time Federal Express investigated the use of Concorde as a supersonic parcel carrier, but this also came to nothing.

The Select Committee, charged to look into Concorde affairs, had to face some rather unpalatable truths. No more Concordes would be sold, the funding of the manufacturers would bring no return to the Governments, and the two airlines concerned did not seem able to operate Concorde profitably. It had been asked to make recommendations specifically on the question of costs due to be met out of the public purse. Was there, it tried to answer, a case for continued expenditure, which although unjustifiable in financial terms, might confer other benefits on the UK, such as prestige or the basis for starting a second generation SST? Then, more sinisterly, from Concorde's point of view, the Committee was to investigate how the cost of immediate cancellation would compare with the cost of continuing and how a proposal to cancel would affect relations between the UK and France.

The Committee heard evidence from representatives of British Airways, the British manufacturers of Concorde (British Aerospace and Rolls-Royce), the Minister of Trade and Industry (Norman Tebbit, an ex BOAC pilot), and the Deputy and Assistant Secretaries of the Department of Industry. Representing Concorde's paymasters, the

Select Committee had every right to question the commercial decisions made by the companies responsible for servicing and operating Concorde.

It appeared that the writing was on the wall for Concorde, the more so since the return of a Conservative Government in May 1979. There is no doubt that they wished Concorde to continue if at all possible, but not at any price.

The change of government in Britain also saw a change of policy towards the nationalized industries. In February 1981, Ross Stainton retired as Chairman of the British Airways Board, and Sir John King took over. He had been charged by the Government to prepare the company for privatisation. Having suffered disappointing financial results, attributable to the world recession, the moment had arrived to study every aspect of the airline with the view to cutting costs and increasing revenue. Nevertheless, the new leadership was more keen than the old on retaining Concorde.

All too frequently large organisations become conscious that their staff can lose a sense of identity and pride in their work. Following the period of recession, the restoration of morale in British Airways was regarded as a most important part in its march back to profitability. To this end, 'profit centres' were set up within the airline. One such centre was the Concorde Division. In May 1982, Captain Brian Walpole, who had been Flight Manager Technical was

Opposite, top The Concorde Fatigue Specimen at the Royal Aircraft Establishment (RAE), Farnborough. Although fully visible, here the airframe was festooned with ducts connected to a hot air supply in order to simulate the heating and cooling experienced by a Concorde on a supersonic flight. Each 'flight' was minutely monitored by computers. With sufficient experience to allow Concordes to fly well into the 21st century, this specimen was dismantled in 1985

Opposite, below The Concorde Fatigue Specimen engulfed by its thermal duct. The thinness of the wing tips and top of the fin meant that they would not suffer significant thermal fatigue, hence they were not under test. The fuel tanks were filled, the cabin pressurised and jacks were used to 'load' the airframe as on a real flight

The BA 195 being prepared for service at Heathrow on a winter's evening. Later, from the west, the sun will rise on this Concorde for the second time in the day

First Concorde to Pittsburgh!

Concorde is frequently chartered to destinations all over America. On this occasion, two weeks after the unveiling of the new livery, Concorde was used to publicise the opening of the Jumbo service between London and Pittsburgh via Washington

Opposite, top Washington Dulles, September 1985, passengers disembarking from G-BOAA via the 'Mobile Lounge'. Once loaded the lounge is lowered prior to driving to the terminal building. After a 50 minute turn round the aircraft will be en route to Miami

Centre Concorde G-BOAA inaugural service to Miami from London via Washington, 27 March 1984. The 1 hour 20 minute sector from Washington to Miami is flown at subsonic speeds over land then at supersonic speeds over the sea south of Wilmington, North Carolina

asked by Gerry Draper (BA Commercial Director) to become General Manager of this new division. As his assistant he brought with him another Concorde pilot, Senior First Officer W. D. (Jock) Lowe. Broadly they divided their responsibilities into two, Walpole looking into ways of increasing revenue and Lowe at ways of reducing costs. The appointment of practising pilots to these positions represented a welcome change from tradition. However, it must be stated that their predecessors in Commercial Division had worked very hard for Concorde's success in conditions which had not been easy. At that time Concorde passenger loads were falling from their peak in 1979 while costs consistently exceeded revenue.

Within months of their new appointment Concorde was faced by a new crisis. In August 1982 Ian Sproat (MP) wrote to Sir John King stating the Government's intention to cease funding the British manufacturers support costs for Concorde and asking British Airways if it wished to take on this responsibility. If BA were to decline, in the words of Keith Wilkins (Head of Planning, BA): 'The supersonic project would terminate.' Termination in Britain at this stage would probably have meant termination in France as well. The date set for this was 31 March 1983.

President Mitterand, unlike his predecessor, did countenance a review of Concorde's financial performance when he came to power in 1980 and Concorde was on the agenda of the Anglo-French summit of 1981. However, at no time in Concorde's history had Britain and France both shared the same opinion regarding cancellation, hence its survival. In Britain at this time, the

Government perceived that by 1983 or 1984 the 80:20 agreement might even be producing a return from which the support costs could be financed, especially since the cancellation of the Singapore route. But Government involvement of this kind was not within the philosophy of the Conservative party in power. Probably for this reason, rather than from wishing to stop Concorde, did Ian Sproat write to Sir John King stating the Government's intention of ceasing to fund the British manufacturers.

*See page 73.

*An Air France
Concorde being
prepared for service
at Kennedy in
October, 1985. By
1984 Air France
Concorde operations
became profitable on
the Paris New York
route. Runway 22R is
one of those preferred
for a Concorde take-
off on the basis of
restricting noise (see
page 60). There are
no similar restrictions
for Concordes
landing at Kennedy

The BA reply indicated that they were very willing to examine the possibility of taking over the support costs, but they would have to be given time to examine the implications. The Government agreed to another year being made available before the axe would finally fall on public money funding the British manufacturers. In the meantime a Department of Trade and Industry Review Group headed by Mr Bruce MacTavish of the Civil Service, would negotiate with BA for the handing over of the Government's responsibility to BA. The BA negotiating team were led by Mr Keith Wilkins (Head of Planning), with Captain Walpole (General Manager Concorde Division), Jock Lowe (Planning Manager Concorde), Sandy Sell (Engineering), and Peter Brass (Accounting).

The team's first job was to find out whether Concorde could make a sufficient operating surplus to fund the British manufacturers' support costs. Their second, and no less important, task was to analyse the manufacturers' activities with a view to reducing costs without impairing service, especially in areas of flight safety. This would rule out any development work not called for jointly by manufacturers and BA. The team were modestly optimistic that Concorde revenue which, had, in the period 1979/80 to 1982/83 been dropping, would improve as the recession passed. Over optimism was not only unwarranted, but might have upset the negotiations. Equally too much pessimism might have brought the negotiations to an untimely end. It took eighteen months to find a satisfactory formula.

The main points at issue were the terms surrounding the acquisition by BA of Concorde spare parts owned by the Government (and useless to anyone other than a Concorde operator), the winding up of the 80:20 agreement soon expected to give government a small dividend, and the replacement of the Government by BA in the contracts with the British manufacturers (British Aerospace and Rolls-Royce). On this particular issue it was fundamental that BA could withdraw unilaterally from the Concorde project at its own discretion without having to finance the British manufacturers if Air France continued Concorde operations. BA made it clear to the Government that they would not pay for the continuation of the operation of the test rig at Farnborough. This had been a major element in the support costs and by 1984 the

full-scale Concorde structure had experienced sufficient 'flight cycles' for the Concordes to continue, at their present rate of use, well into the next century*. In the end BA took responsibility for the dismantling of the rig.

The funding of Concorde's French manufacturers would not necessarily be altered by the proposed changes in Britain – that was a French matter. Hitherto the French manufacturers had received payment from the French Government. In the early 1980s the French Government had promised Air France that it would bear a higher proportion of its Concorde operating loss. In return it reserved the right to dictate where Air France operated Concorde. With the result that the Rio de Janeiro, Caracas and Mexico through Washington routes were abandoned leaving Air France a single daily return Concorde service between Paris and New York. In 1984 Air France operations became profitable.

In April 1983, as discussions between BA and the Government continued, a 30 minute documentary programme about Concorde appeared in the QED series of BBC1. I was technical consultant to the producer, Brian Johnson, and was present as First Officer to Brian Walpole on the London to New York

service which was filmed. (The Flight Engineer on that sector was Senior Engineer Officer Bill Johnstone.) Brian Walpole, during an interview on the programme, made it very clear that Concorde in future would have to stand on its own two feet: 'I believe it can, and, given a reasonable response from Government, Concorde will continue.' Although the tide had started to turn in favour of Concorde before the transmission of that programme, it was from that moment that Concorde ceased to be regarded as a loss maker. Gone were the tiresome yet familiar gibes about its poor prospects.

Slowly and inexorably the negotiations eroded the major outstanding differences between the Government and BA. In the end a sum had to be agreed which BA would pay to the Government for all the Concorde spares, Concorde G-BBDG (202) which was grounded at Filton minus engines and much equipment, the Farnborough Concorde test structure, as well as buying its way out of the 80:20 agreement. In March 1984, eighteen months of detailed analysis were brought to a swift conclusion. In a meeting lasting not more than a quarter of an hour, reminiscent of bargaining in an eastern bazaar, Gordon Dunlop (Finance Director of BA) and the Government representatives agreed on a figure: £16.5m. Concorde was saved.

Great credit is due to the people whose determination found a way of preserving this unique aircraft in service. In particular, Bruce MacTavish as negotiator for the Government and Keith Wilkins astute leader of the BA team deserve great praise. Brian Walpole's and Jock Lowe's infectious enthusiasm and dedication to Concorde were great motivators throughout. During all the negotiations Concorde continued in service thanks to everyone connected with the operation maintaining faith that somehow Concorde would have a successful future.

A Conservative Government spawned Concorde and ensured its right to life through an unbreakable treaty with France in 1962. Twenty-one years (and a few months) later, another Conservative Government severed almost all its financial connections with Concorde; the supersonic airliner had come of age. With expanding charter services and improving figures on the scheduled routes (London to New York and London to Washington and Miami), the commercial future of Concorde in British Airways looked bright.

Overleaf Concorde *G-BOAG, the first of the BA Concordes to be refurbished in the new livery by Landor, April, 1985*

The Flight - Acceleration

The flight deck. The two control columns with their familiar 'ramshorns' shape can be seen. To the right is the Flight Engineer's panel. The nose and visor were down when this picture was taken during a period of servicing in the hangar. Unpowered, the instruments display red failure flags

'Ladies and gentlemen. This is the First Officer, Christopher Orlebar,' comes the voice on the cabin address system. 'We are climbing through 20,000 ft and are just accelerating through the cruising speed of a Jumbo jet: Mach 0.85, 550 miles per hour. We are flying over the track of Brunel's Great Western Railway – another great engineering project – towards Bristol, and in particular Filton, from where this Concorde first flew in 1979.

'The time in New York, if you would like to reset your watches is five minutes to six. We expect to arrive in New York at a quarter past nine. Having left London at ten thirty, you do not need to be an Einsteinean physicist to work out that that will make us one and a quarter hours younger by the time we arrive at Kennedy airport. Although we travel backwards in time it is not sufficiently far to call our destination by any of its original names – Idlewild, or New Amsterdam.

'In six minutes from now we shall be switching on the after-burners. You will feel two small nudges as they come on in pairs. They give extra thrust to the engines to overcome the increased air resistance found during supersonic flight. We accelerate and climb, and by 43,500 ft we shall have achieved Mach 1.7, at which point the after-burners will be switched off. In case there are no thermodynamicists among you I will explain why. By Mach 1.7 the engines will have become very much more efficient due to the increase in airflow through the intakes, which precompress and slows down the air before it enters the engines. There is then sufficient thrust to overcome the increased air resistance caused by those shock waves which appeared just below Mach 1. We continue to climb and accelerate, reaching Mach 2 just above 50,000 ft. Thereafter we climb gently as we use the fuel and so become lighter, maintaining Mach 2, or thereabouts, until we reach today's ceiling of about 58,000 ft – in any case not above 60,000 ft which is as high as we are allowed to fly.'

Another voice now, this time in the headsets of the crew, from the Air Traffic Controller at West Drayton: 'Speedbird Concorde one nine three, London. You are cleared to climb at the acceleration point. Cross eight degrees west at or above flight level four three zero (43,000 ft).'

'Roger. Cleared to climb at the accele-

system, which allows landings in visibilities down to 200 metres (656 ft) with a 'decision height' (whether to land or to go up again) of 15 ft (4.5 metres). Whatever the weather at the destination, the aircraft must be able to divert to an alternate airfield whose weather would allow an ordinary manual landing. The weather at the en-route alternate airfields is also checked. These might be needed in the event of engine failure when Concorde would be forced to decelerate to

Senior Flight Engineer Tony Brown (left), Captain John Massie (centre), and the author at the flight briefing in the Queen's Building at Heathrow

ration point. Cross eight degrees west flight level four three zero or above. Speedbird Concorde one nine three,' comes the reply to London Air Traffic Control. Soon Concorde will be travelling at almost two and a half times the speed of a Jumbo jet.

Two hours previously the three flight deck crew of BA 193 assembled in the Queen's building at London's Heathrow Airport.

'One hundred [passengers] booked. You have Alpha Foxtrot on stand Juliet 2.' Armed with this information and a list of the six cabin crew members, the three crew consisting of Captain, First Officer and Flight Engineer go to be briefed. They study the weather, the fuel flight plan and other relevant information concerning airfields, navigation aids and route information.

The weather forecast at the destination and alternate airfields is of fundamental significance. Is fog likely? Concorde is fitted with a Category Three automatic landing

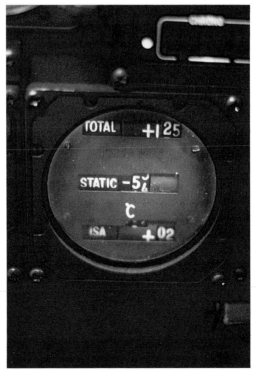

Air temperature gauge on Concorde at Mach 2. The outside air temperature is shown in the 'static' box. The tip of the nose in the 'Total' box and the deviation from the International Standard Atmosphere in the 'ISA' box

subsonic speeds where the range is not so great.

The forecast winds between 50,000 ft and 60,000 ft are studied. They are usually less strong than the winds found up to 40,000 ft. Very rarely do they exceed 100 knots. On average they blow from the west at 30 knots. Cruising at 1,150 knots true airspeed, a 100 knot headwind has less effect on Concorde than on a Jumbo which cruises at 480 knots. Over a 2,000 nautical mile (nm) distance a 100 knot headwind gives Concorde a ground speed of 1,050 knots increasing the flight time by 10 minutes, but a Jumbo with a ground speed of 380 knots would take 65 minutes longer over the same distance. The tracks followed by subsonic aircraft over the Atlantic are varied from day to day to take account of the winds. The supersonic tracks, however, are fixed by the minimum distance consistent with over-water flight where the sonic boom is acceptable.

The temperature to be found at altitude is also of importance. The average over the Atlantic constantly varies, but is of the order of minus 55°C (−67°F) at Concorde's cruising level. A few degrees warmer and the fuel requirement is greater and vice versa. For efficiency the engines prefer cold air. There is a greater mass of oxygen in a given volume of air at a given pressure, in cold air than in hot air.

The fuel required to carry 10 tonnes of payload (100 passengers and their luggage) and 15 tonnes of spare fuel over the 3,150 nm between London and New York is typically 77 tonnes (depending on winds and temperatures). Nevertheless the fuel flight plan is meticulously checked. For taxiing at London 1.4 tonnes are added bringing the total to 93.4 tonnes – some 2 tonnes short of full tanks. The expected take-off weight with these figures is 180 tonnes. The expected flight time on this journey is 3 hours and 23 minutes.

Equipped with the paperwork the crew are driven to the aircraft on stand Juliet 2. At this stage the gleaming paintwork showing off the new British Airways Concorde livery (unveiled 25 April 1985) is somewhat hidden by hordes of service vehicles, fuel bowsers, luggage and catering trucks and transport vans. The passengers congregating in the special Concorde lounge glimpse the unique supersonic nose serene above the white-overalled activity beneath.

It is almost impossible for the passenger, viewing all this activity, to imagine just how many lifetimes of thought and effort

Concorde at 'Juliet 2' during refuelling

preceded this moment of sublime anticipation: flying the world's only successful supersonic airliner. Yet as these words are written, powered flight by men in heavier than air machines has happened well within the lifespan of many living people and commercial supersonic flight is 10 years old.

The 'safety' checks having been completed in the cockpit, the pilots remain on board while the Flight Engineer checks the exterior of the aircraft. He will inspect, amongst other things, landing gear, tyres, engine intakes and the elevons (the flying control surfaces) to the rear of the wing, which look, without hydraulic pressure, rather like flaps in the 'down' position. As he does so he steps over power cables,

refuelling hoses and the high-pressure air hoses for use during engine starting. Finally he rejoins the pilots going through their 'scan' checks. Lights, instruments and audio warnings are all scrutinised. 'Pull up, pull up!' says an insistent microchip from the loudspeakers. It is the terrain avoidance system under test. Another voice, taped and transmitted from the tower, announces: 'This is Heathrow information Romeo, zero eight one five weather, wind two nine zero degrees, one five knots . . .' The data is copied down, relevant for calculating whether conditions are suitable to allow 180 tonnes of Concorde to take-off from runway 28 left (the southerly of the two west facing runways at Heathrow).

Although more crowded with instruments than other airliners, the cockpit in Concorde is equipped with the familiar ones: altimeters, airspeed indicators, artificial horizons and engine temperature and pressure instruments. However, the Machmeters are calibrated up to Mach 2.4, and on closer inspection switches and gauges of systems unique to Concorde become apparent – engine air intake controls, primary and secondary engine nozzle indicators and a centre of gravity meter – but despite diligent searching, there are no flap and slat levers. To the untutored eye it is as foreign and daunting as a cathedral organ is to the tone deaf. But to the crew it is like home; a place that both gives and demands nurture.

'Good morning gentlemen.' It is the Cabin Services director introducing himself to the flight deck crew. The cabin, with the new 'space-age grey' upholstery, has been meticulously checked by the six cabin crew, as has the food and drink to be consumed during the flight. However well the aircraft is operated technically, it is the cabin crew who must supply the ambiance and good feeling that will make the passengers say: 'We had such a good flight . . .' Dedicated to Concorde they meet the challenge. They are lucky since they can see the fruits of their dedication – satisfied passengers. But the cabin crew are trained in other equally vital tasks affecting the well-being of the passengers; they must be experts with all the emergency and survival equipment that is carried on board.

No less dedicated, but behind the scenes, are the thousands of individuals who have made the flight possible. The shifts of engineers, the refuellers, the catering staff, the Chairman, the ramp controller, the Chief

'Number four uplifted four quarts,'

'No performance A.D.D.'s, but there is a history on number two H.F. radio, it is very slow to tune.'

'Speedbird Concorde one nine three, cleared to New York Brecon one foxtrot, squawk two one zero three, track Sierra Mike.'*

*See end papers.

'Cleared to start, one two one nine for push'.

The clearance is read back by the crew to the tower.

'Fifty three and half for take-off with a burn-off of 900 kilograms' comes another statement. It is akin to the tuning up of an orchestra.

The Captain or First Officer may fly the aircraft. Today it is the First Officer's turn, so the Captain acts as co-pilot to the First Officer although he retains overall command. Thus the captain reads the 'before start check list'. Henceforward all actions are co-ordinated between the three crew as a team, and each one, where possible, monitors the other's actions.

'Altimeters' says the Captain.

'QNH one zero one five set, eighty, six eighty, normal and 20 ft on the radio altimeter' comes the reply. Later: 'INS one, two and three'. Concorde is navigated by three inertial navigation systems (INS). Once programmed with the latitude and longitude of the starting point of the aircraft, they will continually read out the aircraft's position. Programmed with a route (a series of turning or 'way-points') the auto-pilot will steer the aircraft along that route. All three computers are checked.

'ASI bugs and pitch indices' says the Captain. 'Vee one, one six zero; rotate, one nine five . . .' These are the relevant take-off speeds. The first one, 160 knots, is the decision speed. Up to this speed the aircraft may safely stop within the runway distance; beyond, the take-off may be continued safely even with one of the four engines out of action. On this journey the aircraft will be 'rotated' (that is pitched up) to 13 degrees at 195 knots (225 mph) to become airborne at 217 knots (250 mph).

The loadsheet is checked. Ninety of the one hundred passengers have turned up and are on board; there are ten 'no-shows'. The zero fuel weight and the zero fuel centre of gravity have been programmed into the relevant computer. They are finally checked. Fuel is shifted or 'burnt off' prior to take-off to position the centre of gravity to one specific point. With no tailplane, the precise

The 'elevons' drooped without hydraulic pressure

Executive, the tractor driver, the administrators . . . the list goes on. Their roles are vital, their aim identical – the successful flight of British Airways aircraft. That Concorde performs so well is proof that great pride in the job exists with this section of British Airways. Success breeds success; the 'Halo' effect of Concorde benefits all sections of the airline.

Familiar calls can now be heard.

'OK for boarding?'

'Fuel book,'

position of the centre of gravity on Concorde is more important than for an aircraft with a tailplane.

Finally: 'Start engines'. The inboards are started first. All four on, even at idle power, might damage the towbar on the tractor during the push-back. Hydraulic pressure from pumps driven by the engines at 4,000 lb per square inch (psi) is fed to the flying controls. They spring into life, ready for the comprehensive 'flying control check' that follows. The hydraulic jacks are signalled electrically, but have a mechanical back-up channel. The electrical signals are modified by an auto-stabilisation system which reacts similarly to the reflex actions in a human. The outboard engines are started, the tractor and towbar unhitched, communication with the ground engineer is cast off and Concorde taxis towards runway 28 left.

'Good morning, ladies and gentlemen. This is the First Officer adding my words of welcome to those of the Captain. I would like to describe the take-off, with an apology to those of you who already know our procedures so well. There is a greater thrust to weight ratio on Concorde than there is on subsonic aircraft so the take-off is a bit more sporty, if I can put it that way. One minute and twenty seconds after the start of the take-off run we shall be reducing the thrust and switching off the after-burners, which have been adding to that thrust. This reduces the noise near the airport. Inside the cabin you will notice both a reduction in noise and in the angle of climb. By about twelve minutes after take-off we shall be flying at 95 per cent of the speed of sound – Mach 0.95. Once we clear the coast of South Wales we shall accelerate to Mach 2. The weather in New York is perfectly satisfactory for aviators but not good for sunbathers – it is raining, but the forecast is for it to clear by our time of arrival.'

'Speedbird Concorde one nine three cleared for take-off runway two eight left,' transmits the controller from the tower at Heathrow. 'Roger cleared for take-off, Speedbird Concorde one nine three,' replies the Captain.

All the checks are complete.

'Three, two, one, now.'

On the 'now' the throttles are opened and the stop watches started.

'Speed building,' calls the Captain, then 'One hundred knots.'

'Power checks,' responds the engineer. Each engine is using fuel at over 20 tonnes per hour and giving 38,000 lbs of thrust with after-burner.

'Vee one'. The First Officer moves his hand from the throttles, to the control column. There is no stopping now.

'Rotate', the control column comes back and the whole aircraft rotates to an angle of 13 degrees above the horizontal. Concorde becomes airborne at 217 knots.

'Vee two' – a safe climbing speed in event of engine failure.

Captain Meadows, one of the original BA Concorde pilots, carrying out the preflight 'scan' checks. Each item is checked one after another following a strict pattern

'Positive rate of climb.' Now there is at least 20 ft between the wheels and the ground.

'Gear up,' commands the First Officer. The Captain selects it up.

'Two forty knots', the pitch attitude is raised from 13 degrees to nearly 20 degrees to maintain 250 knots. Then looking to the stop watch the Captain calls 'Three, two, one, noise.'

On the word 'noise' the engineer switches the after-burners off and adjusts the throttles to a preset position on the throttle quadrant. To maintain 250 knots with less thrust the angle of climb must be reduced. The First Officer pushes the control column gently forward to maintain a new attitude of 12 degrees to the horizontal. The rate of climb reduces from 4,000 to 1,200 ft/min.

At 7 nm from London more power is applied and the speed is allowed to rise consistent with crossing a radio beacon called Woodley (close to Reading) at 4,000 ft or higher. Accelerating out of 250 knots the nose and visor are raised. In compensation for diminished view of the outside world a glorious calm settles on the flight deck, free from the aerodynamic buffet of the lowered nose and visor. By 300 knots the flight becomes smoother as the buffet from the 'vortex' lift disappears. There are no flaps and slats on Concorde, the same wing-shape serves throughout Concorde's 1,000 knot speed range.

'Speedbird Concorde one nine three,

Concorde has a cabin crew complement of six. Here the Cabin Services Director is accompanied by three stewardesses in summer uniform, in a Concorde recently refurbished in the new 'space age grey' upholstery

climb and maintain flight level two eight zero,' says the London Air Traffic Controller. The clearance to climb is acknowledged by the Captain; 28,000 ft is programmed into the autopilot. The indicated airspeed during the climb is 400 knots. It is also as fast as the aircraft is allowed to fly between 6,000 and 32,000 ft, the limit being shown by a black and orange chequered pointer on the airspeed indicator. Climbing at a constant indicated airspeed into the thinner air

The initial cruising altitude out of London is 28,000 ft. Note Mach number: Mach 0.95. The compass shows TRUE course as opposed to magnetic. Note the drift about 7° right with a strong southerly wind

Overleaf Concorde landing at London Heathrow in new livery (from a painting by Michael Turner)

The 'Marilake' indicators showing the progress of the flight. For short periods they are also programmed to show the distance to go to the destination

rearward movement of the centre of gravity by about 2 ft, achieved by shifting the fuel. By the time Mach 2 is reached the centre of gravity will have been moved aft by a further 4 ft.

The autopilot 'acquires' at 28,000 ft. As it does so the auto-throttles switch in and take responsibility for maintaining the speed – Mach 0.95 (385 knots indicated airspeed at this altitude), 100 mph faster than most subsonic aircraft.

'Speedbird Concorde one nine three cleared cruise climb, flight level four nine zero to six zero zero.' The message is acknowledged and 60,000 ft is programmed into the autopilot.

'Checks complete down to the after-burners; fuel is going aft; one mile to go,' says the Engineer. The First Officer pushes the throttle fully forward. A signal is sent to the engines, via their controlling computers, to give maximum climb power. The distance 'to go' shows zero.

'Inboard reheats' . . . a nudge as they light up increasing the thrust by about 20 per cent.

'Outboard reheats,' . . . another nudge. Each engine is now burning fuel at over 11 tonnes per hour. The Mach number climbs and hovers on Mach 1. The shock wave passes the static pressure-ports on the side of the fuselage causing a fluctuation on the pressure driven instruments, notably on the vertical speed indicator. Mach 1.01 is

means that the Mach number will rise. At 25,000 ft it will have risen to Mach 0.93 – the limit for a subsonic climb. At that point there will still be about 70 nm to go before the coastline – the acceleration point. Once clear of the coastline, Concorde can accelerate to a Mach number which would cause the sonic boom to be heard. Usually the boom does not reach the surface until Mach 1.15 is achieved, a figure dependent on temperatures and winds.

'Centre of gravity steady at 55 per cent' the Engineer intones. As the Mach number builds the centre of lift starts to move to the rear. This has to be compensated for by the

The pilot's view of the instruments during Mach 2 cruise. At 53,000 ft the indicated airspeed is 501 knots although the true airspeed is 1,150 knots as evidenced by the Machmeter. Concorde climbs gently throughout the cruise as the weight reduces. The rate of climb in this picture is about 500 ft/min

indicated and Concorde is supersonic.

At Mach 1.3 the variable ramps inside the engine air intakes begin to operate. They arrange the shock waves formed in the intake mouth in the most efficient pattern possible to compress and slow the airflow down prior to its entering the engine face.

The acceleration becomes more rapid as the Mach number builds. The passengers watch the progress on the 'Marilake' indicators at the front of each cabin. At Mach 1.7 a barely perceptible lurch indicates that the after-burners have been switched off. Reference to the cabin indicators shows the aircraft to be climbing through 43,500 ft, the outside air temperature to be minus 52°C (−62°F) and the ground speed 1,120 mph. There is a 20 mph headwind. Acceleration is now less rapid. Forty minutes from take-off Mach 2 is attained at an altitude of 50,200 ft and lunch is served.

'Ladies and gentlemen, at the risk of interrupting the Marriage of Figaro on the inflight entertainment – or worse still, your conversation,' says the First Officer, 'We are cruising at Mach 2 (a mile every $2\frac{3}{4}$ seconds) and climbing gently towards twice the height of Mount Everest – 58,000 ft. Here at the threshold of space, the sky above is far darker, almost black and the view of the Earth's horizon just betrays the Earth's curvature. Today it is very clear but big

volcanic eruptions in any part of the world, throwing up tons of minute fragments of debris into the upper atmosphere, can reduce the clarity.

'The sun is now climbing from the west. In winter it is possible to leave London after sunset, on the evening Concorde for New York, and watch the sun rise out of the west. Flying at Mach 2 in an easterly direction at these latitudes will cause the sun to set in the west at three times its normal rate, casting, as it does so, a vast curved shadow of the Earth, up and ahead of the aircraft.'

Mercifully the passengers do not choose Concorde solely to observe astronomical phenomena whilst eating haute cuisine served by the dedicated cabin crew. They fly on Concorde because it saves them days, not hours. West-bound, the critical working hours of the day are preserved; east-bound, the purgatory of the overnight sector is avoided. Concorde only flies between London and the United States during the waking hours of the Atlantic Seaboard dwellers.

Two hours out of London, Newfoundland is visible on the right-hand side. The passengers visit the flight deck. Foreign secretaries, famous people, chief executives, pop stars, owners of publishing empires, financiers and Concorde admirers, who have just come to experience 20th-century air travel at its most supreme, are among the

Newfoundland from 55,000 ft. The earth's curvature is clearly visible although slightly exaggerated in this picture. The sky above is almost black here on the threshold of space

Senior Engineer Officer Bill Johnstone demonstrating that the gap to the rear of the engineer's panel is wide enough to accommodate a hand when the fuselage has expanded, due to its having been heated by the airflow at Mach 2

passengers. All are treated as VIPs.

Some are stunned into silence. Then 'Do you know what each of these switches and dials do?' 'No,' replies the First Officer, 'We only have them to preserve the mystique,' laughter, then: 'Does Concorde really grow eight inches during the cruise?'

The engineer explains that due to the compression and friction of the air, the temperature of the outer surface of the fuselage rises to about 100°C (212°F), hence the expansion and increase in length. He puts his hand into a gap between his panel and bulkhead; it fits. 'Once the fuselage is cool there is no space to do that. If you want two flights on Concorde leave your hand there during the deceleration, it will become trapped. The only way then of removing it would be to wait for the next supersonic flight. It would be painful, but it might be worth it!' he adds with a grin.

Should the temperature on the nose, the hottest point, be about to exceed 127°C (260°F), then the Mach number has to be reduced. This occurs when the outside air temperature becomes warmer than minus 50°C (−58°F). The speed of sound is greater in warmer air so the reduced Mach number has little effect on the flight time.

'Boston this is Speedbird Concorde one nine three heavy flight level five six eight.' (56,800 feet.) A small cross with BA 193, FL 568 and 999 appears on the controllers radar screen. The 999 refers to Concorde's ground speed, the radar is calibrated no higher, so cannot show the 1,120 knots registered in the cockpit.

'Speedbird Concorde one nine three heavy. Roger. I have you radar identified. Omit position reports.' (The suffix 'heavy' serves to differentiate groups of aircraft, on the basis of maximum allowable take-off weight.)

Concorde is passing the south-western end of Nova Scotia now. The track is being precisely steered by the autopilot following instructions from the inertial navigation system (INS). A small yellow light captioned 'R Nav' illuminates in the top right hand corner of the Captain's instrument panel. Nantucket DME (distance measuring equipment – a radio pulse beacon), over 250 nm away, has just taken over the refinement of the almost impeccable accuracy of the inertial navigation system. Travelling at 1,900 ft per second the position is known to within about 2,000 ft.

The end of the supersonic cruise is near.

Engine instruments on the centre panel. Each vertical row of five gauges applies to one engine, there are yet more on the engineer's panel. Note the fuel flows, they total about 20 tonnes/hr. To the lower right, the INS shows the position in latitude and longitude. The left hand one shows distance to go to the next turning point and the time to go in minutes, 334 nm in 18.5 minutes. Gander DME, (refining the INS position) was 176.1 nm to the north when the picture was taken, as shown by the readout on the right of the picture. Note the readings of temperature, altitude, indicated airspeed and Mach number

CONCORDE

Concorde has a cabin
crew of six, their
dedication to
Concorde as indeed
everyone connected
with Concorde has
been fundamental to
the success of
commercial
supersonic flight

MACH
2·00

Some of the snippets
of information
appearing in the
'Marilake' passenger
display screens
placed on the
bulkhead to the front
of each of the cabins.
During the cruise the
Mach number is 2.00;
from time to time the
plasma screens show
the distance to go
derived from the
aircraft's navigation
system (See top
photograph on page
92)

WELCOME
TO
CONCORDE

TEMP
-11°C

MENU

PERITIFS & COCKTAILS

Sweet and Dry Vermouth
Campari Soda
Americano · Negroni
Medium Dry Sherry
ry Martini · Gin · Vodka
y · Old Fashioned · Manhattan
—Whisky · Gin · Brandy
Gin Fizz

hisky · Brandy · Gin · Rum

agne Cocktail

ITS

Bourbon · Rye

RINKS

ck and white

us

ge to

CONCORDE

London · New York

APERITIFS · CHAMPAGNE

Canapés
Caviar, veal galantine, kumquat with herb cheese

LUNCH
Déjeuner

MAYONNAISE DE SAUMON
AUX POINTES D'ASPERGES
Fresh poached salmon garnished with cucumber, asparagus spears
and mayonnaise

HOMARD À LA CRÈME DE ROQUEFORT
Maine lobster poached in white wine and herbs, topped with a delicate
creamy blue cheese sauce. Served with leaf spinach and baby carrots

SUPRÊME DE POUSSIN GRILLÉ
Grilled breast of grain-fed chicken
served with leaf spinach and baby carrots

ASSIETTE FROIDE
As a lighter alternative may we suggest our prime roast fillet of beef
garnished with horseradish-flavoured potato-salad, fresh asparagus,
watercress, tomato and lettuce

SALADE COMPOSÉE
Seasonal salad featuring apple, red and yellow peppers
served with piquant vinaigrette or avocado and lime dressing

PECHE POCHÉE AU CHAMPAGNE
A fresh peach poached in champagne, flavoured with vanilla
and served on a bed of strawberry mousse
Decorated with a fresh mint leaf

PLAT DE FROMAGES
Selection of English Stilton and Cheddar cheese with Swiss Emmenthal
Served with celery and crackers

CAFÉ · CAFÉ DÉCAFÉINE
Coffee or decaffeinated coffee served with a selection of quality
chocolates

BRITISH AIRWAYS

LONDON—NEW YORK

3h40

Haute cuisine at high altitude and grande vitesse

The cabin interior in flight

MPH 1020

THANK YOU

FOR FLYING CONCORDE

CONCORDE

Flight Certificate

Presented to

_____

who flew supersonically on Concorde between

_____

on

_____

Colin M Marshall
Chief Executive.

Captain Brian Walpole
General Manager, Concorde Division.

The Flight - Deceleration

'Speedbird Concorde one nine three heavy, Boston, cross three nine four three north seven one zero seven west at flight level five two zero or above, cleared to cross Linnd flight level three nine zero or above. Descend and maintain flight level three nine zero.' The descent clearance is read back. Concorde must cross the boundary of a 'warning' area, dedicated to military flying, above 52,000 ft, before entering the regular airways system at a point over the ocean called Linnd at 39,000 ft or above, but no lower – yet.

The deceleration and descent distance is calculated; typically 120 nm are covered from Mach 2 to Mach 1. Decelerating over the ocean en route to New York, the point at which the deceleration is started is dictated by the distance required for nearly the whole descent. On most other routes it is fixed by the need to be subsonic 35 nm before any coastline sensitive to sonic booms; on those occasions Concorde decelerates through Mach 1 level at 41,000 ft;

into New York Concorde becomes subsonic during the descent through 35,000 ft.

There is a sharp noise: it is a microchip's rendering of a 'wake-up!' bugle call. The crew are carrying out the 'Deceleration and Descent Checklist'. The first item is to test the warnings associated with the autopilot disconnecting itself – hence the alerting audio warning. Next come the radio aids required for the landing and the procedure for climbing out again, if the landing is aborted for any reason. The altitude to which it is safe to descend and the whereabouts of the high ground or buildings are scrutinised. Finally the crew adjust their safety harnesses.

'Ladies and gentlemen, in 200 miles – 10 minutes in Concorde, but half an hour for the Boeing 747 in the 100 knot headwind which it is experiencing beneath us – we shall be commencing our deceleration. The time in New York is twenty past eight in the morning. We shall be landing at five past nine, on runway four right – the right hand of the two north-east facing runways. The rain has cleared and the temperature is 70°F.'

Thrust is reduced to an intermediate setting. Too low a value might cause the engines to surge (backfire); alarming, but not dangerous; also the racks of computers would overheat if the air conditioning supplied by the engines failed to supply a sufficient cooling draught.

There is a whiff of ozone. Between 40,000 ft and 60,000 ft Concorde has been flying in an ozone rich atmosphere. At 'cruise power' the compression of the air in the engines heats the air to over 400°C (750°F). This converts all the ozone present in the compressor into oxygen. The air bled from the engines prior to its being cooled in the air conditioning system is thus free of ozone. At reduced power, the compression and heating are less – hence the trace of ozone. In spite of the huge temperature drop in the supply of air to the air conditioning system, there is no temperature variation in the cabin.

At Mach 1.6 there is a further thrust reduction. Once the indicated airspeed has dropped to 350 knots the descent commences: 350 knots at 58,000 ft corresponds to a Mach number of 1.55 (890 knots true airspeed); by 35,000 ft it will correspond to Mach 1*.

The engineer moves the centre of gravity forward to keep the aircraft in trim. He pumps fuel from a tank in the rear of the aircraft to tanks in the fuselage and wings. Eight or nine tonnes of fuel are moved forward at this stage. The gap between his panel and the bulkhead closes and the warmth radiating from the windows reduces as the fuselage cools.

Further descent clearance is acknowledged: 'Roger New York, cross three five miles south-east of Sates at one two thousand feet, altimeter two nine eight four.' The altimeters are adjusted to show altitude referenced to the pressure at sea level, 29.84 inches of

The view of Cape Cod and Nantucket Island on the weather radar. The track takes Concorde to the south of the coast line, the deceleration commencing 50 nm to the south of Nantucket. The weather radar's primary role is the detection of thunderstorms, but it plays a useful part in confirming the aircraft's position

The three crew members at work. In the foreground is Senior Flight Engineer George Floyd

*See the 'Flight envelope' in Appendix.

mercury. Hitherto, they have shown altitude referenced to a standard pressure of 29.92 inches of mercury (1,013.25 millibars) – hence the instruction to maintain 'flight levels'. A flight level of 350 corresponds to 35,000 feet with the altimeter referenced to the standard pressure setting of 1013.25 millibars.

'Concorde one nine three, traffic eleven o'clock five miles south-west bound – one one thousand feet.' The crew peer slightly left and below. 'Contact, Speedbird Concorde one nine three.' 'Contact' means that the other aircraft has been seen – nothing worse. Although air traffic controllers are primarily responsible for the separation of aircraft under their charge, the crew include a careful lookout as part of their cockpit routine. The view ahead, although the visor is raised, is surprisingly good.

As the speed falls the angle of attack must be increased to maintain the lift. 'Angle of attack' is not some kind of refined military manoeuvre; it is the angle between the aircraft and the oncoming air (see page 11). As it is increased so the view of the airspace directly ahead of the pilots becomes progressively obscured by the nose. By 250 knots the visor and nose must be lowered for adequate vision ahead to be maintained. Initially the nose is lowered to five degrees. On final approach, where the angle of attack is 14 degrees, the nose is lowered to its fully down position (12.5 degrees).

'All secure aft,' the chief steward reports. This means that he has checked that all the passengers are strapped in and the cabin equipment is stowed ready for landing.

'Ladies and gentlemen, this is the First Officer. We are under the control of the New York radar controller and will be landing in eight minutes from now.'

'Speedbird Concorde one nine three, fly heading three five zero degrees to establish on the localiser runway four right, maintain 2,000 ft until established, reduce to two one zero knots.' The instruction is acknowledged, and the aircraft turns while 210 knots is dialled into the 'auto-throttles' and the 'IAS acq' button is pressed. As the speed falls below 220 knots the drag increases, calling for a thrust increase. Concorde is unique among airliners in flying at speeds below its minimum drag speed.

A short 'bugle call' is heard. The First Officer has disconnected the autopilot. Today he will carry out a manual landing. 'Localiser active,' calls the Captain. The radio beam defining the path to follow to the runway has been approached. The aircraft must be turned to the right from its heading of 350° M (referenced to Magnetic north) onto one that will let it track precisely along the radio beam transmitted from the ground. There is a crosswind from the right so the aircraft heads 48° M (3° east of north-east) to track 43° M along the localiser beam of runway 4 R.

By 12 miles to touchdown the speed has been stabilised at 190 knots. 'Glideslope active,' calls the Captain. There are 9 miles to touch down. 'Gear down and landing check-list please,' calls the First Officer. The engineer reads the checklist. There is a double thump as the main undercarriage legs lock down, almost simultaneously. Four green lights appear confirming that all four have been extended – two main, one nose and a tail gear.

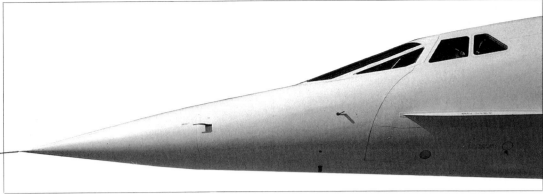

Nose and visor up

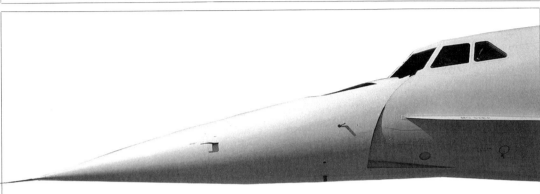

Visor down, nose 5 degrees

'Nose,' says the engineer.

'Down and green,' replies the Captain, referring, not to the colour of the nose, but to a green light which confirms that the nose is locked down. The view of the runway is now quite unobscured.

'Glideslope engaged,' calls the Captain. Concorde will now follow a second radio beam, this one slopes towards the landing point making an angle of three degrees with the horizontal. Together the two radio beams, glideslope and localiser, are called the Instrument Landing System (ILS). The word 'glide' here is a misnomer. No jet aircraft could glide at such a shallow angle to the horizontal with all the drag from its flaps, least of all Concorde, with the high 'induced' drag found when the slender delta wings are asked to give lift at slow speed. It is a powered approach. A speed of 190 knots is maintained through use of the auto-throttles.

The First Officer follows two yellow bars which form a cross over his artificial horizon. The horizontal one commands him to pitch the aircraft either up or down to maintain the 'glideslope'; the vertical one, to turn either left or right to follow the 'localiser'. The bars are signalled by the automatic flight control system. Had the autopilot been engaged it would have pitched and turned the aircraft to follow the two radio beams.

'One thousand foot radio,' calls the Flight Engineer. This is the height of the main-wheels above the surface, determined by bouncing a radio wave off the surface. It is a far more precise measurement of height than that available through the pressure alti-meter; however, it only works below 2,500 ft. So well does it measure the height of the aircraft above the ground that the aircraft performs incredibly smooth automatic land-ings, somewhat to the chagrin of the pilots.

'Beep, Beep, BEEP, BEEP, Beep, Beep' in the headsets.

'Marker, height checks,' says the Captain. This is in response to this audible radio beacon being overflown at the correct height – 920 ft. The veracity of the glideslope has been checked – a little academic with the runway so clearly in view, but vital in conditions of low visibility.

'Eight hundred feet radio,' calls the Flight Engineer. Now the speed is reduced from 190 knots to the speed required just over the threshold of the runway, 163 knots at a landing weight of 103 tonnes. Concorde decelerates during the descent from 800 ft (2.34 nm before touchdown) to 500 ft (1.34 nm before touchdown). To maintain 163 knots, more power is required than was needed at 190 knots. The procedure is called the 'reduced noise approach', because less thrust is needed throughout the approach down to 500 ft. First because the drag is less

Opposite The Flight Engineer's panel showing the fuel management system. In the centre there is the centre of gravity metre showing 58.8 per cent (a measure of its position with respect to the Aerodynamic Root Reference Chord – see page 106), half way along the chord would be 50 per cent; one per cent corresponds to about one foot. The white pointer must lie within the two orange limit pointers (marked FWD and AFT) in order to maintain aerodynamic balance. The tank at the rear has 9,810 kg of fuel in it. This will be moved forward to central tanks during the deceleration. The total fuel on board is showing 34,000 kg. In this picture each engine has used about 15,000 kg

View of runway 4R
at JFK from about
1000 ft on final
approach over the
lowered nose and
visor

—200 feet —

—100 feet—

Crossing the runway
threshold. The wheels
are still at 50 ft
above the ground
with the pilots
another 37 ft above
them

at 190 knots than at 163 knots and secondly because less thrust is required during the period of deceleration. The noise generated by the engines is less with less thrust, and the fuel consumption is lower. Had an automatic landing been carried out, the final approach speed would have been achieved by 1,200 ft above the surface, so stabilising the descent rate for a longer period to allow the landing computer to make a smooth touchdown.

During final approach Concorde consumes fuel at ten times the rate per mile than is the case towards the latter end of the supersonic cruise. At the intermediate speeds the fuel consumption is also much higher; hence the requirement to arrive with 15 tonnes of spare fuel, enough for 50 minutes in the stacking pattern prior to a landing.

'Speedbird Concorde one nine three heavy, cleared to land four right wind zero seven zero at one five knots,' says the controller in the Kennedy tower. Rarely is Concorde held up by congestion at this hour in the morning.

'Cleared to land Speedbird Concorde one nine three heavy,' acknowledges the Captain.

'Five hundred feet,' calls the Flight Engineer. It is somewhat reminiscent of a 19th century sailor calling out the depths he has plumbed ('By the mark ten').

'Stabilised', confirms the Captain. The auto-throttles have captured the final approach speed – 163 knots and Concorde is established in the correct position for landing.

'Four hundred feet,'

'One hundred to go,' responds the Captain

'Three hundred feet,'

'Decision height,' calls the Captain.

Landing clearance has been received, the runway is visible and clear of obstacles. 'Continuing,' responds the First Officer. A 'go-around' is possible right up to the point of touchdown.

The approach lights on runway four right

protrude out of the water of Jamaica Bay. 'Two hundred feet,' and the pilots are 37 ft higher than the main wheels. 'One hundred feet'; over dry land now. 'Fifty', the autothrottles are disconnected. 'Forty, thirty, twenty, fifteen.' The throttles are manually closed. At this point the aircraft would be pitched forward, both by the pressure of air trapped between it and the runway, referred to as 'ground effect', and by the reduction in thrust, but the First Officer gently checks this tendency by bringing the control column back to hold the attitude constant as the descent rate decays in the increasing ground effect. He also pushes the left rudder pedal to lose the remaining three degees of drift required to fly down the centre of the runway, caused by the crosswind. Now the main wheels track along the runway for a moment before they touch.

A puff of smoke and dust whisks from each set of main-wheel tyres into the two vortices, one over each wing: a clear indication of the nature of the airflow that has been supplying lift during the final stages of the approach. Idle reverse thrust is selected whilst the next manoeuvre is carried out – landing the nose wheel; during this the flight deck has to descend a further 17 ft.

'Stick forward,' calls the First Officer. The nose-wheel is down, and reverse thrust is selected. There is a roar in the cabin – noisier than at take-off. The brakes are applied. The stopping appears urgent, but all is normal. 'One hundred knots,' calls the Captain. Outboard engines are selected to idle reverse. 'Seventy five knots', and the inboards go to idle reverse. 'Forty knots groundspeed,' all engines are selected to forward idle thrust.

'After landing check, shut down two and three,' says the First Officer. The nose is selected to five degrees, unnecessary systems are switched off, the two inboard engines are shut down and the Engineer pumps four tonnes of fuel into the front tank to ensure that the aircraft will not tip tail down during unloading.

'Left at the end, cross one three left, right on the outer and call ground point nine,' says the controller. It is a kind of pidgin English, meaningless to the uniniated, but totally clear to the crew. Over the maze of concrete and tarmac that constitutes John F Kennedy Airport, New York, the crew find their way to the British Airways Terminal, at a speed no faster than a mile every two and three quarter minutes.

'Ladies and gentlemen, welcome to New York.' This time it is the Captain addressing the passengers.

'Our maximum altitude today was 58,000 ft and our maximum speed 1,320 mph, giving an average over the whole distance of close on 1,100 mph. On behalf of all the crew thank you for flying with us on Concorde; we look forward to seeing you all again. Finally, the Jumbo jet that left 10 minutes before us from Heathrow is very nearly, but not quite, half way here.'

A marshaller waving two fluorescent wands directs Concorde over the last few feet. The wands cross, the aircraft stops.

'Parking checklist,' says the First Officer.
'Brakes,' responds the Engineer.
'To park,' replies the First Officer.

The checklist continues, like some litany. The passengers disembark. 'Mind your head sir as you leave' cautions the Cabin Services Director, standing at the forward door to bid 'au revoir' to the passengers. They have had an excellent flight.

The landing sequence. Concorde G-BOAF landing on runway 4R at Kennedy. Note the vortices, the landing of the nosewheel and the buckets (secondary nozzles) closed over the jet pipes to deflect the jet efflux forward at an angle of about 50° to the horizontal to give reverse thrust. Since the aircraft tends to pitch up with reverse thrust selected the stick is held forward, thus the elevons move down, as can be seen. The nose is in its fully down $(12\frac{1}{2}°)$ position for the landing, once the landing run is complete it is selected to 5°

The Future

Concorde has now carved a viable niche for herself in the airline transport market, but when the idea of building a supersonic transport was first mooted, the resulting aircraft was supposed to be able to match the economics of the existing long range subsonic aircraft. Even the cabin of the SST was to be divided into First and Second (or economy) Class. However the appearance of the Boeing 747 in 1970 with its much lower seat mile costs, put an end to that idea; an 'economy' class fare on Concorde would have been far higher than on the B747. Thus Concorde has just one class, superior to anything else. Yet surprisingly Concorde has entered the charter market with enormous verve and success, about a tenth of the annual passenger total comes from this source. The Cunard shipping line in particular were quick to catch on that there were just two great ways of crossing the Atlantic, the QE2 being one and Concorde the other. A substantial part of Concorde charter work is in association with Cunard. Now that Concorde has become a profitable aircraft, carrying close on 100,000 passengers per year (BA Concordes had carried 794,000 passengers by mid 1985*), it is pertinent to ask whether an Advanced Supersonic Transport (AST) will appear in the future, and if so, how can it be financed?

Almost as soon as a design for an aircraft has been fixed and its manufacture started, better ways of building it become apparent. After the big American airlines turned down their Concorde options in 1973, the Concorde project was reviewed to see if a superior Concorde could be developed from the existing design. The manufacturers proposed to incorporate weight saving measures, extra fuel tanks, a better engine and an improved wing from the 15th production aircraft onwards. Seeing only financial loss if these improved Concordes were put on sale at realistic prices, $40m–$47m (at 1974 prices), the Government declined to fund the improvements. Soon after Concorde entered service there was another proposal to improve the aircraft, including the retrofitting of existing Concordes with a foreplane or 'canard'. This proposal also came to nothing. Sadly Concorde has not had the benefit of gradual

Concorde G-BOAG, The Red Arrows and the QE2 over the English Channel, Summer 1985. Captain John Hutchinson, noted for BBC television commentary for major British Air Shows, was on board on this occasion, with Captain Leney (Flight Manager, Technical) at the controls. Very many Concorde charters have been organised by Cunard – hence the publicity value of this association

*Air France Concordes had carried 612,590 passengers by October 1985.

A Concorde
passenger at Kennedy

Various American
AST designs based
on the 'Arrow'
planform. Note the
preference for a
tailplane, European
designs favour a
canard

enough to avoid risking unpredictable costs that might, for instance, be associated with the development of special techniques or materials. Above all the economics of the AST must be sufficiently attractive to ensure a reasonable production run of, say, 500 units.

The history of science and technology is one of gradual evolution punctuated by the appearances of substantial breakthroughs. In aviation the introduction of the internal combustion engine making manned flight in heavier than air machines was one such breakthrough. The invention of the jet engine, the discovery that a slender delta could generate vortex lift and the appearance of the microchip, were others. The AST could be developed by extending well tested techniques or, at some risk, by venturing to search for new ones.

Not surprisingly research and development in aeronautical engineering has continued since Concorde, both in the general field of aviation and with an AST specifically in mind.

On the subject of aerodynamic efficiency, work in the 1970s both in Europe and America has suggested that vastly improved L/Ds (lift to drag ratios) throughout the speed range of an AST, compared to Concorde, could become a reality. Consider for instance, the L/D of Concorde at speeds below 250 knots – the speeds flown shortly after take-off, or when holding, during manoeuvring prior to landing and particularly during a diversion. Under these conditions Concorde's L/D is about 4 compared to a 'conventional' aircraft's at 8 to 9. This results in a very heavy rate of fuel usage from engines whose efficiency is far from optimum at the low speeds. For example Concorde normally arrives at New York with 15 tonnes of spare fuel (about $1\frac{1}{2}$ times the payload weight), $2\frac{1}{2}$ tonnes against possible contingencies and $12\frac{1}{2}$ for a diversion. To arrive with 15 tonnes of spare fuel in New York, approximately 30 tonnes must be loaded in London. (In other words fuel is used in order to carry fuel). An improvement in the low speed L/D to about 6, so that the New York reserve requirement could be fulfilled by arriving with 11 tonnes, would reduce the spare fuel increment of the uplift from 30 to 22 tonnes.

This improvement could be translated into one, or a mixture of, a greater payload, more range or a way of reducing noise. The noise after take-off is reduced, when the aircraft is lighter either because it can climb

evolution as is the case with most long service aircraft.

In spite of much of its design being fixed by the late 1960s and early 1970s – the pre-microchip era-Concorde is nevertheless an absolutely superb achievement. If given the go ahead now for an AST it is relevant to ask what attributes it would need to have to be successful and whether they could be developed.

The AST must have sufficient range to be able to reach Anchorage (Alaska) from Western Europe, a range of the order of 4,500 nm. With a refuelling stop at Honolulu this would open up many Pacific destinations. It must not suffer a penalty to its range when, through sonic boom considerations, it is cruising at subsonic speeds. It must be quieter on take-off and landing than Concorde. It would need a passenger capacity which reflected the fare levels it could realistically demand on suitable routes. It must have a speed which is fast enough to be productive – in terms of revenue producing miles per day – yet slow

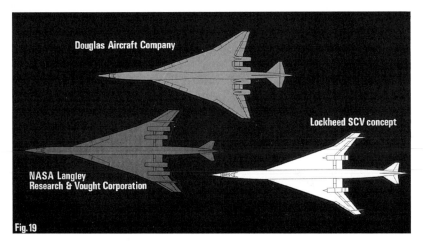

Douglas Aircraft Company

Lockheed SCV concept

NASA Langley
Research & Vought Corporation

Fig. 19

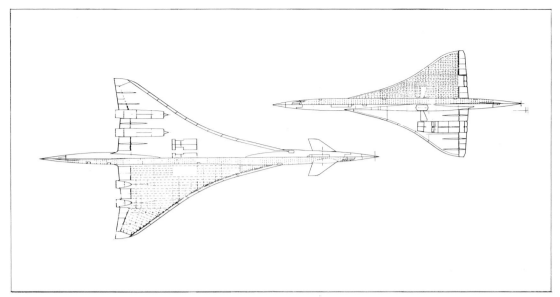

Concorde and an AST proposal

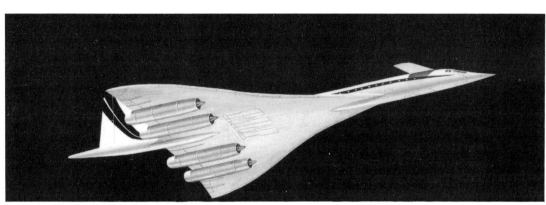

An artists impression of the AST from the plan above. Later proposals used a more exaggerated arrow planform

A three-quarter view of the 400 seater AST based on an 'arrow' planform with a blended fuselage. Passengers in the rear would have television pictures of the outside world.

Although only twice the take-off weight of Concorde, this design would carry four times the number of passengers. Whether the seat mile costs would be low enough to make the aircraft viable to sell in sufficient numbers to recoup the development investment is open to question

Two designs for an AST. The upper version carrying 275 passengers, the lower, 400. Note the presence of a canard. As the design weight exceeds about 650,000 lb, engine silencing becomes progressively more difficult, unless a variable cycle engine is developed

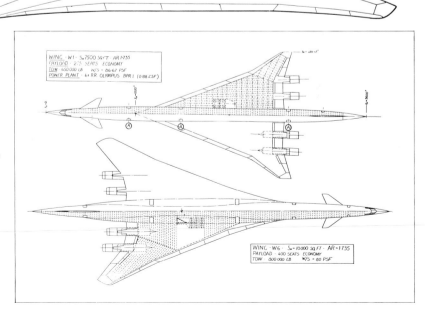

more steeply, overflying any noise sensitive areas at greater altitudes, or because it can reach 'standard' altitudes with less thrust. The noise after take-off would also be less since, with an improved L/D, less thrust would be required to overcome the reduced drag. This example slightly over simplifies the case since the L/D improvement would have to be 'bought', to some extent, by high lift devices themselves having some weight, but it demonstrates the principle. Also for simplicity the AST has been presumed, in this example, to have similar engines to Concorde.

Such an improvement in the low speed L/D would follow from two techniques. One from aerodynamic devices such as retractable 'slats' on the leading edge of the wing, and the fitting of a canard. The canard, as well as partially or totally taking over responsibility from the elevons for control of the aircraft in pitch, would also give a lift force near the front of the aircraft. This force would have to be balanced by the elevons going down slightly, thus behaving as flaps.

The second technique involves computers. If the centre of gravity is moved well to the rear the nose pitches up, as it would were there a canard, the elevons must go down in compensation, thus adding to the 'flap' effect. In this way the size and weight of the canard can be minimised. However the aircraft with such a rearward centre of gravity would be quite unstable. To make the aircraft flyable, the flying controls would have to be 'active'. In other words the control surfaces would move as a result of electrical signals generated by an autostabilisation computer as well as from inputs from the pilot. Such controls were pioneered on Concorde, but not to the extent that Concorde is unflyable through instability should they fail, furthermore a conventional mechanical signalling link to the hydraulically-powered controls is retained on Concorde. In a 1981 research programme in Britain a Jaguar aircraft flew successfully with no mechanical signalling back up channel, to its quadruplexed digital active control systems. Later flights in-

vestigating yet more unstable configurations, with the centre of gravity well to the rear, proved the effectiveness of the system.

An AST to be successful would need an improved cruise L/D compared to Concorde's $7\frac{1}{2}$. An 'arrow' planform – like a delta but with the centre portion of the trailing edge moved forward – would give an L/D of 10 or even 11. But without a tailplane or canard this shape does not allow for adequate control in pitch, hence it was not applied to Concorde. Thus designs for ASTs always include a canard or a tailplane.

If it were possible to improve the cruise L/D there would be a variety of advantages, for example a mixture of more range, less noise and more payload would be available.

Regarding propulsion for the AST, ideally a variable cycle engine should be developed. This would behave as a by-pass engine to give fuel efficient and quiet propulsion at subsonic speeds, but becoming, by means of internal air valves, a turbojet engine for efficiency at supersonic speeds.

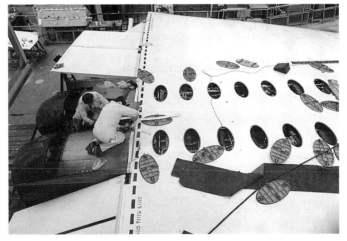

Concorde inspires great dedication and enthusiasm among all those whose privilege it is to contribute to the supersonic operation, not least from the maintenance engineers – the unsung heroes of the Concorde Story

For flight testing electronic flying control systems, this Jaguar aircraft has a modified wing planform and a centre of gravity so far to the rear as to make the aircraft unflyable without autostabilisation through 'Active' controls. An AST would rely heavily on this kind of technology.

The Rolls-Royce RB211 engine is an example of a by-pass engine. Air enters the first stage of the compressor before being divided into two concentric streams. One stream passes through the engine core, itself like a turbo jet engine but having an extra turbine responsible for turning the shaft on which the first compressor or 'fan' stage is fixed. The other stream by-passes the engine. Since five times as much air by-passes the RB211 core as goes through it, it is said to have a by-pass ratio of 5:1. At speeds in excess of Mach 1 an engine with a large by-pass becomes unuseable due to its large frontal area, which causes excessive drag, and its low velocity jet efflux which gives insufficient thrust. The turbo-jet engine on the other hand becomes progressively more efficient at supersonic speeds (up to Mach 3) and it gives plenty of thrust at low speeds, albeit somewhat

inefficiently and noisily due to its high speed jet efflux. Hence the attraction of an engine which can vary its 'cycle'. Such an engine, called the 'hybrid fan' is under consideration by Rolls-Royce for use in a supersonic vertical take-off military aircraft.

At the annual meeting of the AIAA (American Institute of Aeronautics and Astronautics) in Washington in 1985, Richard Peterson (Director of NASA's Langley Research Centre in America (National Aeronautics and Space Administration)) struck a pioneering note by envisaging an AST with over 5,000 nm range (Concorde's maximum is about 3,700 nm) powered by two variable cycle engines. Use of laminar flow control (see page 16), he noted, could increase the range of the AST to over 8,000 nm, and reduce by half the 'over pressure' from the sonic boom. Whether this would make it acceptable over populated land is open to question. But caution prevails on the European side of the Atlantic, where a powerplant derived from the Rolls-Royce Olympus engine is preferred. This engine would have a small by-pass ratio with half as much air going round the engine core as through it (0.5:1). Turbine blade technology – the materials from which they are made and their method of cooling – has improved since the design of the Olympus 593 was frozen. Then, a by-pass ratio on a supersonic engine would have made the engine less efficient; by 1985, however, technology had improved sufficiently to allow a 350°C (662°F) increase in turbine entry temperature. If such an engine could be fitted to Concorde, then 40 per cent more payload (about 4 tonnes) could be carried between London and New York, or a combination of improved range and/or payload would be available.

Unlike the variable cycle engine this mini-by-pass Olympus derivative would require an engine silencer. Various organisations, led by Rolls-Royce and McDonnel Douglas, contributed to an engine noise suppression programme which included flight testing an HS 125 which had one engine fitted with an 'ejector suppressor'. The system consisted of lobes over the jet pipe and a shroud with an acoustic lining surrounding the jet efflux to the rear. Good results were reported from tests. If applied to an engine on an AST the lobes would have to be retractable and arranged in such a way so as not to interfere with the variable convergent/divergent nozzle system that would be necessary for supersonic flight. A

An HS 125 with the
left-hand Rolls-Royce
Viper turbo-jet
modified to test
various engine
silencer designs

One of the
configurations tested
during investigations
into engine silencing
by Rolls-Royce and
McDonnell Douglas

certain amount of development work, with attendant risks, would be needed before this scheme could become operational. Noise suppression on approach to landing could be achieved by arranging the approach to be flown whilst constantly decelerating to the touch down speed. Thus the high drag associated with low speed does not have to be overcome with thrust. This technique was pioneered with Concorde, which, in good weather, decelerates to landing speed during the latter stages of the approach.

On the subject of materials for the structure, titanium alloys, about which much was unknown in the 1950s have been improved. Richard Peterson's AST would be built using the new methods of working with titanium known as superlastic forming and diffusion bonding. A titanium alloy would comfortably cope with the skin temperatures associated with Peterson's target cruise speed, Mach 2.7. Whether plastic composites will be capable of withstanding long periods exposed to high temperatures is not clear. European thinking on the subject of materials is more cautious. Some advocate a maximum speed defined by a 100°C total temperature limit. This corresponds to about Mach 1.85 over North Atlantic latitudes and would add about 10 minutes to Concorde's flight time between London and New York. This would have the advantage of using techniques proven by Concorde.

The microchip revolution has largely taken place since Concorde design was finalised. Computers now help enormously not only in the design stage of an aircraft, by optimising design work, but also on board the aircraft. By the mid-1980s many subsonic aircraft were flying with television

screens relaying computer generated data and images of the aircraft's navigational situation and the state of the various systems – such as the electrical generation and hydraulic power systems. The weight and complexity of the wiring can be reduced dramatically with the introduction of a 'data busbar' – effectively a single wire carrying quantities of information to various computers, in the same way that a single wire connects the television to the home computer. Concorde's engines are controlled by no less than 52 computers, some analogue and others digital. Although they work

Opposite
The Rolls-Royce
RB211 engine. The
by-pass flow exits
around the engine
core. The frontal area,
evident by the size of
the by-pass duct,
would cause too
much drag at
supersonic speeds
and the jet velocity
would be too low to
give effective
propulsion

HOTOL
This projected unmanned space vehicle could be the basis for the world's first generation sub-orbital transport. Lift to drag ratios at very high speeds in the thin atmosphere above 100,000 ft would not affect the efficiency of this craft, since for periods of the flight it would have little weight, becoming weightless (but not mass-less) for a short period prior to reentry. Its big cross sectional fuselage minus the mass of fuel would be a positive advantage during reentry, slowing it down before it became as hot as denser vehicles, like the Space Shuttle, become.

The propulsion system would use atmospheric oxygen when available, switching to an on-board oxygen supply for the space portion of the flight. A sub-orbital derivative might not need to carry its own liquid oxygen supply

Ariane 1/200 scale

Shuttle 1/200 scale

1/100th scale model of HOTOL

astonishingly well, digital computers alone could now reduce the number required to about 10.

The technology of the mid-1980s is more than equal to the task of building a successor to Concorde provided that not too much reliance has to be placed in the appearance of breakthroughs. A safe design would be for a 250–300 seater with about 4,500 nm range (more as it evolves) travelling at Mach 2. No aerodynamic solution to alleviate the sonic boom seems possible yet, so boom sensitive land would still have to be avoided – having sufficient supersonic range combined with subsonic efficiency is the only solution here. The money to develop such a craft is also

available. The only piece of the jigsaw missing, is the excuse (or reason) that would have to be found to justify the cost of development. Having started the programme, there remains the risk that seat mile costs, projected to be higher than contemporary subsonic aircraft, might not be achieved due to unforeseen technical difficulties. As there still appears to be no military requirement for an aircraft with similar qualities to an AST, no development would not come from that quarter. There is, however, one technological 'joker' in the pack, and that is HOTOL.

HOTOL is a acronym for horizontal take-off and landing. It is not intended to be an aircraft, but rather a space-shuttle replace-

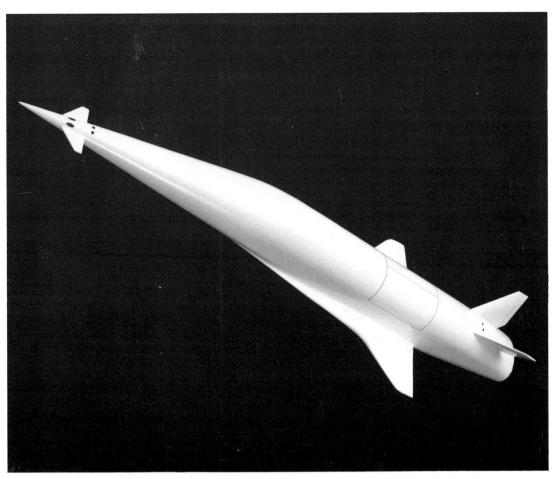

The line diagram of HOTOL does not show the intake about which information was not originally divulged. Shown inset is the model displayed at the Paris Air Show of 1985. This gives some impression of what the engine intake might look like. However, the precise method by which the thrust unit(s) use either atmospheric or liquid oxygen has not, at the time of going to press in 1985, been published

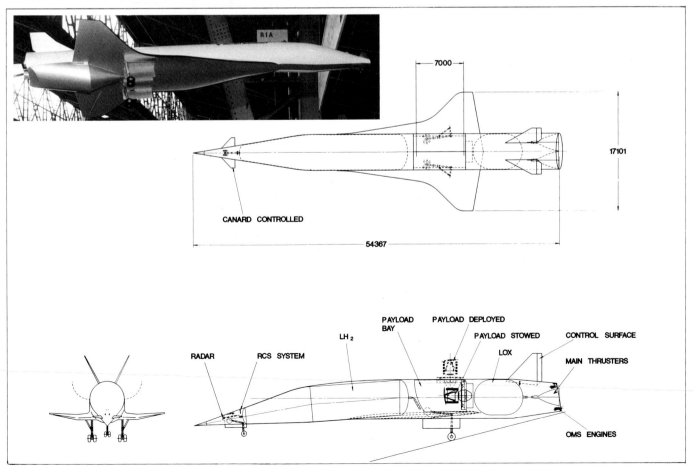

CANARD CONTROLLED

7000

17101

54367

RADAR   RCS SYSTEM   LH₂   PAYLOAD BAY   PAYLOAD DEPLOYED   PAYLOAD STOWED   LOX   CONTROL SURFACE   MAIN THRUSTERS   OMS ENGINES

ment. It is under consideration by British Aerospace Dynamics, but, by 1985, has yet to be given a Government go-ahead. Unlike the Space Shuttle, this unmanned vehicle would take-off horizontally leaving behind its 'take-off' undercarriage. For the atmospheric portion of the climb its thrust unit would burn atmospheric oxygen with the fuel, resorting to on board liquid oxygen as the atmosphere becomes too thin on its way into earth orbit. This would obviate the necessity of having, as the Space Shuttle does, a vast external unreusable fuel tank and two solid fuel rocket boosters – reusable only after their collection from the ocean and refurbishment. Return from orbit in HOTOL would be similar to the Space Shuttle, but due to its size and relatively light weight without fuel, compared to the Space Shuttle, slower and therefore experiencing lower skin temperatures than the Shuttle. Just prior to landing it would deploy its own landing undercarriage.

Government money could one day be forthcoming for such a programme, either as part of the defence budget or as British involvement in a unique space programme that promised an alternative to other launch systems. HOTOL could be made ready for relaunch more quickly than the Space Shuttle with correspondingly lower costs.

A manned derivative of HOTOL could carry a load of passengers from Europe to America in half an hour, Australia in an hour. There would be no sonic boom generated during the space or 'sub-orbital' portion of the journey. For a few moments the passengers would experience weightlessness. This speed would probably represent the physical limit of terrestrial travel.

Whatever the next major aerospace programmes are, they will need men of the stature of Sir George Edwards, Sir Stanley Hooker and their like, to see them grow, blossom and bear fruit. There is no doubt that one day it will be possible for a fare paying passenger to circumnavigate the world in ninety minutes, it is just a question of matching technological advance with sufficient courage and vision to usher in new eras of transport. Mankind has been developing new and faster modes of transport since the beginning of the industrial revolution, so it is very unlikely that he will stop doing so just as he approaches the threshold of the twenty first century AD.

This publicity photograph of four Concordes was taken on Christmas Eve 1985 for release on 21st January 1986 – the tenth anniversary of Concorde's commercial service. Leading the formation was Captain Brian Walpole (General Manager Concorde), commanding the other Concordes were Captains David Leney, John Cook and John Eames.

Proof that supersonic aircraft fulfil a role in the airline business comes from Concorde's continued success

Appendices –

Max take-off weight	185,070 kg (408,000 lb)
Max landing weight	111,130 kg (245,000 lb)
Max weight without fuel	92,080 kg (203,000 lb)
Max payload (approx)	13,150 kg (29,000 lb)
Max number of passengers	128 (but BA Concordes are fitted with 100 passenger seats)
Max fuel at specific gravity 0.800 limited by volume:	95,680 kg (26,400 gallons)

The dimensions of Concorde. The measurement marked with the asterisk is for the 'Aerodynamic Root Reference Chord'. It is used when referring to the position of the centre of gravity moved by the transference of fuel (see accompanying diagram). Thus the centre of gravity on most take-offs (53.5%) is 48 ft 6 in behind the forward point, and 53 ft 6 in at its most rearward (59%) during the supersonic cruise

Range

The maximum range is constrained by several factors including payload, reserve fuel required on arrival, weather conditions and the amount of the route that can be flown supersonically. A typical maximum range on Concorde with 100 passengers plus baggage (10,000 kg total payload) and normal fuel reserves, is 3,500 nm (4,030 sm). The route between Bahrain and Singapore was flown in the colder air found over the tropics; this improved the efficiency of the engines allowing a range of 3,720 nm to be flown regularly. Although the payload limit on this sector was 7,500 kg (75 passengers) it could usually be increased to close on 100 passengers when conditions were favourable. The maximum recorded range on Concorde under very favourable conditions, and therefore difficult to plan in advance, was between Washington and Nice, a distance of 3,965 nm (4,255 sm) flown on 11 September 1984 with 54 passengers in G-BOAB taking 4 hours and 7 minutes.

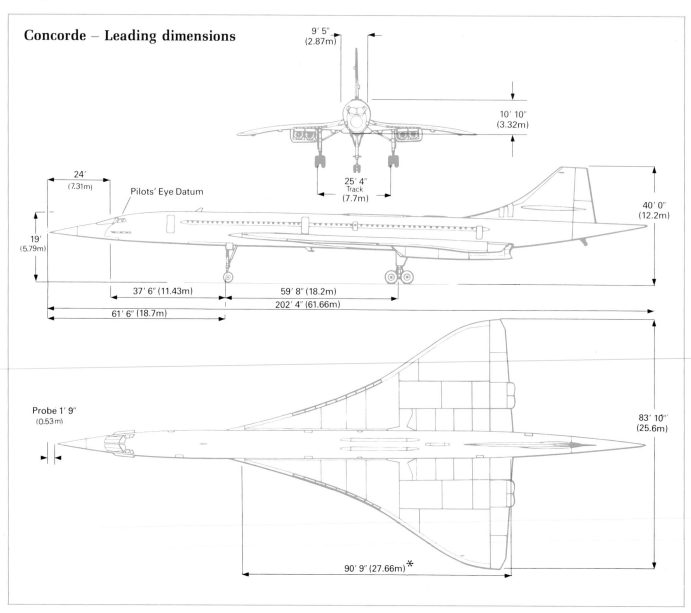

Concorde – Leading dimensions

Powerplant

Four Rolls-Royce/SNECMA Olympus 593 Mark 610 turbo jet engines. Maximum thrust at take-off with afterburner (reheat) contributing about 20% to the total – 38,050 lb.

At take-off 95% of the thrust is delivered by the engine and 5% by the nozzle and intake assemblies

During supersonic cruise only 50% of the thrust is delivered by the engine; the remainder is delivered, equally shared, by the variable ramp assembly and the convergent/divergent nozzle system. The purpose of the diffuser is to slow, and therefore compress, the air, which is now subsonic, still further before it enters the engine face

Note A convergent passage slows and compresses a supersonic airflow, while a divergent passage slows and compresses a subsonic airflow.

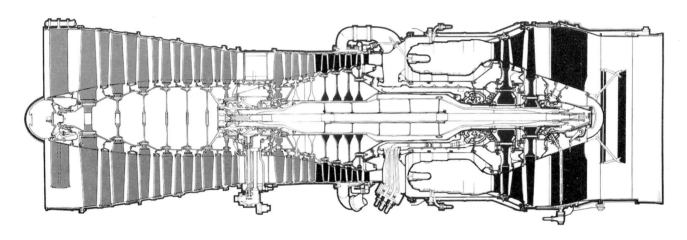

Above The Olympus engine is a 'two-spool' engine. The inner, or low pressure (lp) shaft revolves within the outer, or high pressure (hp) shaft. There are fourteen compressor stages, seven on each shaft, driven by their respective turbines. As the air approaches the combustion chambers, during the supersonic cruise, it becomes very hot due to its compression (over 80:1 total), hence the need to construct the final four compression stages from a nickel-based alloy – usually reserved for the turbine area. (The darker shades, green in the cutaway engine below, show the more heat resistant alloys.) To the rear of the turbines is the reheat assembly. The amount of fuel burnt in the combustion chamber controls the rpm of the hp shaft, whilst varying the area of the primary nozzle (see top) controls, at a given rpm of the hp shaft, the rpm of the lp shaft.

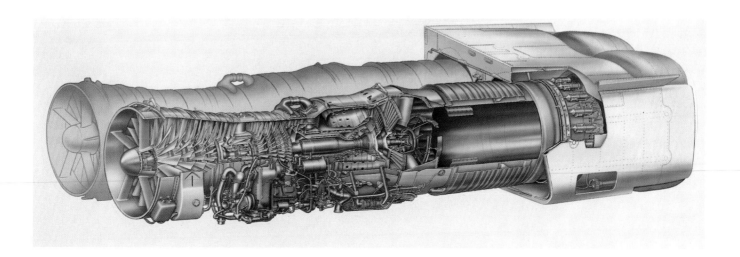

The anatomy of Concorde

Emergency equipment
E1 Oxygen-bottle stowage
E2 Drop-down masks
E3 First-aid oxygen in galley top
E4 Four 36-man life rafts
E5 Chute stowage
E6 Windscreen (electrically heated), hydraulic wipers and fluid rain clearance
E7 Emergency radio
E8 Fire-suppression bottles
E9 Direct-vision panel and exit
E10 Spraymat de-icing

General structure
1 Variable-geometry drooping nose
2 Droop guide-rails
3 Droop hinge-joint
4 Retracting visor
5 Visor guide-rails
6 Visor refracting link
7 Visor jack
8 Outward-opening, plug-type passenger door (66 in × 30 in, sill 16 ft 5 in above ground)
9 Service door (48 in × 24 in)
10 Underfloor baggage hold (pressurised), 26 ft × 38 in × 55 in (308 cu ft)
11 Rear baggage compartment (pressurised), door to stbd (429 cu ft)
12 Middle passenger doors (port and stbd) 73 in × 34 in
13 Metal-faced floor panels
14 Rear emergency door (port and stbd) 68 in × 34 in
15 Light alloy/balsa sandwich floor panels
16 Machined window panel
17 Triple-gap window, removable as a unit
18 Multi-layer windscreen, removable as a unit
19 Forged wing/fuselage main frames
20 Stringer carry-through
21 T-section spot-welded stringers (front fuselage)
22 Z-section spot-welded stringers (rear fuselage)
23 Single-flange frames (front fuselage)
24 Double-flange frames (rear fuselage)
25 Rolled-aluminium RR58 skin
26 Front pressure bulkhead
27 Rear pressure bulkhead and tank wall
28 Spar-box, machined girder side pieces
29 Spar-box, machined cap strip/boom
30 Pre-stretched, integrally machined wing-skin panels
31 Lattice-tube pin-jointed ribs
32 Machined ribs
33 Corrugated, machined tank wall and spars permitting thermal expansion
34 Single-web spars
35 Forged wing (forward tanks) adjustable mountings
36 Pressure-floor curved membranes (to relieve thermal stress)
37 Pressure/passenger floor-support beams
38 Machined pressure-floor support beams over wheel bay
39 Machined, pressurised keel box carrying services
40 Stressed (15 g upward impact) tank roof
41 Vapour seal over tank roof
42 Unpressurised aft systems bay
43 Pressurised forward systems bay
44 Fin support structure (tube and extruded members)
45 Machined fin spars (rivetted to fuselage frames)
46 Removable leading-edge sections
47 Machined ribs
48 Chemically milled skin

49 Expansion joints between sections
50 Removable outer wing (tank 5A, port, and 7A, stbd)
51 Wing fixing by 340 bigh-tensile steel bolts
52 Quick-look removable inspection panels
53 Inspection panels, screw-fixed
54 Honeycomb structure (control surfaces, engine nacelles and intakes)
55 Seat rails
56 Floor supports, permit longitudinal expansion
57 Toilet
58 Galley unit
59 Coat stowage
60 Overhead baggage racks with doors
61 Passenger-service units on underside of baggage racks
62 Pilot heads

Air conditioning
A1 Intake-air tapping to heat exchangers
A2 Primary heat exchanger (one per engine)
A3 Secondary heat exchanger (one per engine)
A4 Heat-exchanger exhaust air
A5 Delivery to cold-air unit
A6 Fuel-cooled heat exchanger (one per engine, both systems)
A7 Cold-air unit (one per engine both systems)
A8 Delivery to cabin air-distribution system
A9 Distribution duct
A10 Riser to distribution duct
A11 Duct to forward risers
A12 Window ventilating air (all windows)
A13 Air-recirculating duct
A14 Individual punkahs on service panels, adjustable to seating arrangement
A15 Cabin-air exhaust through roof filter via trim to under-floor
A16 Heat and sound insulation (glass fibre and polyester sheet)
A17 Baggage-compartment cooling air
A18 Cabin-floor-level exhaust duct to ventilate equipment bays
A19 Flight-deck air duct
A20 Window demisting
A21 Equipment venting air
A22 Equipment-air extraction duct

A23 Automatic discharge/relief valve (normal diff. 10.7 lb/sq in)
A24 Manual discharge valve
A25 Thrust-recovery nozzle
A26 Low-pressure venting air between vapour seal and tank roof
A27 Ground-conditioning connection
A28 Undercarriage-bay cooling air

Controls
C1 Control cable runs under floor
C2 Rod linkage to surface power control units (stand-by linkage, electrics primary)
C3 Power control unit mounting
C4 Electrically signalled, manual stand-by power control unit
C5 Twin output from power control unit
C6 Control-unit fairing
C7 Elevon
C8 Flexible joint
C9 Elevon outer hinges, permit spanwise expansion
C10 Ram-air turbine
C11 Retracting jack

Flight deck
D1 Captain's seat
D2 Second pilot's seat
D3 Third crew member's station
D4 Roof panel
D5 Third crew member's panel

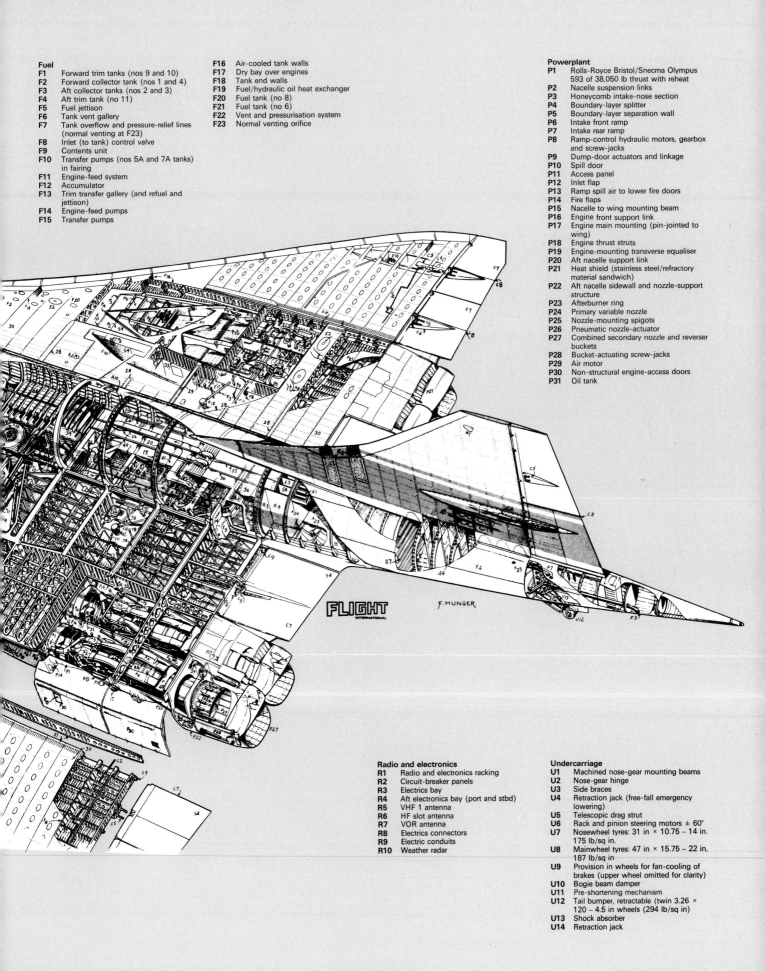

Fuel

F1	Forward trim tanks (nos 9 and 10)
F2	Forward collector tank (nos 1 and 4)
F3	Aft collector tanks (nos 2 and 3)
F4	Aft trim tank (no 11)
F5	Fuel jettison
F6	Tank vent gallery
F7	Tank overflow and pressure-relief lines (normal venting at F23)
F8	Inlet (to tank) control valve
F9	Contents unit
F10	Transfer pumps (nos 5A and 7A tanks) in fairing
F11	Engine-feed system
F12	Accumulator
F13	Trim transfer gallery (and refuel and jettison)
F14	Engine-feed pumps
F15	Transfer pumps
F16	Air-cooled tank walls
F17	Dry bay over engines
F18	Tank end walls
F19	Fuel/hydraulic oil heat exchanger
F20	Fuel tank (no 8)
F21	Fuel tank (no 6)
F22	Vent and pressurisation system
F23	Normal venting orifice

Powerplant

P1	Rolls-Royce Bristol/Snecma Olympus 593 of 38,050 lb thrust with reheat
P2	Nacelle suspension links
P3	Honeycomb intake-nose section
P4	Boundary-layer splitter
P5	Boundary-layer separation wall
P6	Intake front ramp
P7	Intake rear ramp
P8	Ramp-control hydraulic motors, gearbox and screw-jacks
P9	Dump-door actuators and linkage
P10	Spill door
P11	Access panel
P12	Inlet flap
P13	Ramp spill air to lower fire doors
P14	Fire flaps
P15	Nacelle to wing mounting beam
P16	Engine front support link
P17	Engine main mounting (pin-jointed to wing)
P18	Engine thrust struts
P19	Engine-mounting transverse equaliser
P20	Aft nacelle support link
P21	Heat shield (stainless steel/refractory material sandwich)
P22	Aft nacelle sidewall and nozzle-support structure
P23	Afterburner ring
P24	Primary variable nozzle
P25	Nozzle-mounting spigots
P26	Pneumatic nozzle-actuator
P27	Combined secondary nozzle and reverser buckets
P28	Bucket-actuating screw-jacks
P29	Air motor
P30	Non-structural engine-access doors
P31	Oil tank

Radio and electronics

R1	Radio and electronics racking
R2	Circuit-breaker panels
R3	Electrics bay
R4	Aft electronics bay (port and stbd)
R5	VHF 1 antenna
R6	HF slot antenna
R7	VOR antenna
R8	Electrics connectors
R9	Electric conduits
R10	Weather radar

Undercarriage

U1	Machined nose-gear mounting beams
U2	Nose-gear hinge
U3	Side braces
U4	Retraction jack (free-fall emergency lowering)
U5	Telescopic drag strut
U6	Rack and pinion steering motors ± 60°
U7	Nosewheel tyres: 31 in × 10.75 – 14 in. 175 lb/sq in.
U8	Mainwheel tyres: 47 in × 15.75 – 22 in, 187 lb/sq in
U9	Provision in wheels for fan-cooling of brakes (upper wheel omitted for clarity)
U10	Bogie beam damper
U11	Pre-shortening mechanism
U12	Tail bumper, retractable (twin 3.26 × 120 – 4.5 in wheels (294 lb/sq in)
U13	Shock absorber
U14	Retraction jack

FLIGHT INTERNATIONAL

F. MUNGER

The Flight Envelope

How the fuel is used to move the centre of gravity on Concorde. The position of the centre of gravity is measured as a percentage of the 'Aerodynamic Root Reference Chord' (see dimension chart). The position of the centre of gravity restricts the aircraft to a speed range shown by the 'limit bugs' on the Machmeter; or alternatively, at a given speed, the centre of gravity must be within limits shown by 'bugs' on the centre of gravity indicator (see photographs on pages 89, 92 and 100)

Concorde must be flown within the slightly shaded area shown on the graph. The maximum operating indicated airspeed limit (V_{MO}) varies not only with altitude, but also, to a small extent, with Concorde's weight. Above 51,000 ft the maximum operating Mach limit (M_{MO}) over-rules V_{MO}; by 60,000 ft M_{MO} (Mach 2.04) corresponds to 440 knots indicated airspeed. The lowest authorised speed limit below 15,000 ft is not shown on this graph since it is related either to weight on take-off from a particular runway, or to landing weight.

Although M_{MO} is Mach 2.04, Concorde generally cruises at Mach 2. There are, however, further constraints to the speed. One is derived from the position of the centre of gravity; at the furthest forward position of the centre of gravity, the top Mach number limit is Mach 0.8; during the acceleration the centre of gravity is moved progressively rearward and at its most rearward point the Mach number range is from Mach 1.55 to over Mach 2.04; however, the top speed is then limited by M_{MO}, V_{MO} or T_{MO}. T_{MO} is the maximum operating temperature limit, representing another constraint to the speed; the maximum temperature at the nose must not exceed 127°C.

In practice this does not become a limiting factor to Concorde until the outside air temperature is warmer than −50°C, at altitudes above 48,000 ft.

Next to the altitude, in thousands of feet, is shown the outside air temperature corresponding to the International Standard Atmosphere (ISA). Next to this is shown the speed of sound for that given temperature. The true outside air temperature is usually at variance from the 'standard' by a few degrees either way over the North Atlantic, so the figure for the speed of sound must be regarded as approximate. Over the equator, where the tropopause is higher, temperatures between 50,000 and 60,000 ft are of the order of ISA −20°C (i.e. −77°C). At this temperature the speed of sound is 545 knots (627 mph).

The formula for the speed of sound (a) is

$$a = \text{constant} \times \sqrt{\text{absolute temperature}}$$

assuming temperature in °K and speed in knots, the constant = 38.89

For an outside air temperature of −57°C (216°K)

$$a = 38.89 \times \sqrt{216}$$
$$= 571 \text{ knots}$$

The formula for giving the approximate rise in temperature (ΔT) °C for a given speed is

$$\Delta T = \left(\frac{\text{speed in mph}}{100} \right)^2$$

Thus at Mach 2 when the outside air temperature is −57°C the temperature rise is

$$\left(\frac{2 \times 657.5}{100} \right)^2$$
$$\simeq 173°C$$

Under these conditions the total temperature is 173° − 57° = 116°C.

Note At the speeds associated with a Space Shuttle (or HOTOL) re-entering the earth's atmosphere this formula is not applicable.

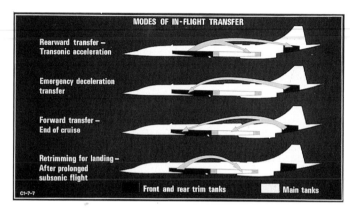

MODES OF IN-FLIGHT TRANSFER

Rearward transfer – Transonic acceleration

Emergency deceleration transfer

Forward transfer – End of cruise

Retrimming for landing – After prolonged subsonic flight

C1-7-7

Front and rear trim tanks   Main tanks

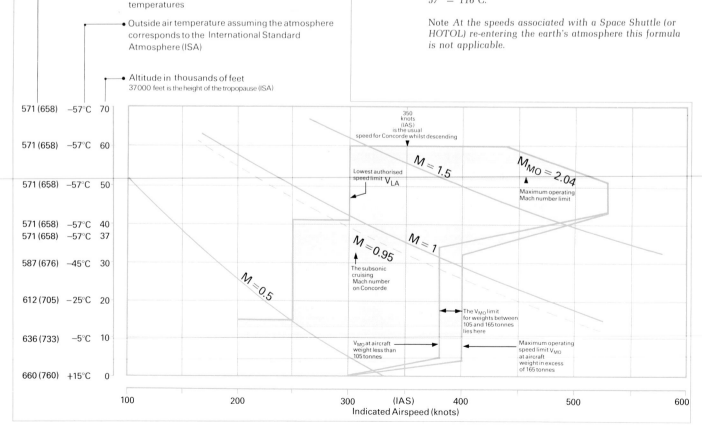

● Speed of sound in knots (mph) at the given temperatures

● Outside air temperature assuming the atmosphere corresponds to the International Standard Atmosphere (ISA)

● Altitude in thousands of feet
37000 feet is the height of the tropopause (ISA)

571 (658)	−57°C	70
571 (658)	−57°C	60
571 (658)	−57°C	50
571 (658)	−57°C	40
571 (658)	−57°C	37
587 (676)	−45°C	30
612 (705)	−25°C	20
636 (733)	−5°C	10
660 (760)	+15°C	0

350 knots (IAS) is the usual speed for Concorde whilst descending

$M = 1.5$

$M_{MO} = 2.04$
Maximum operating Mach number limit

Lowest authorised speed limit V_{LA}

$M = 0.95$
The subsonic cruising Mach number on Concorde

$M = 1$

$M = 0.5$

The V_{MO} limit for weights between 105 and 165 tonnes lies here

V_{MO} at aircraft weight less than 105 tonnes

Maximum operating speed limit V_{MO} at aircraft weight in excess of 165 tonnes

100   200   300   (IAS)   400   500   600
Indicated Airspeed (knots)

The Aircraft

Type	Registration number		First flight	Retired, now at
Prototype	F-WTSS	001	March 69	Le Bourget
Prototype	G-BSST	002	April 69	Yeovilton
Pre-prod.	G-AXDN	01	Dec 71	Duxford
Pre-prod.	F-WTSA	02	Jan 73	Orly
Production	F-WTSB	201	Dec 73	
Production	G-BBDG	202	Feb 74	Filton
Production	F-WTSC[1]	203	Jan 75	
Production	G-BOAC	204	Feb 75	
Production	F-BVFA	205	Oct 75	
Production	G-BOAA	206	Nov 75	
Production	F-BVFB	207	March 76	
Production	G-BOAB	208	May 76	
Production	F-BVFC	209	July 76	
Production	G-BOAD	210	August 76	
Production	F-BVFD	211	Feb 77	
Production	G-BOAE	212	March 77	
Production	F-WJAM[2]	213	June 78	
Production	G-BFKW[3]	214	April 78	
Production	F-WJAN	215	Dec 78	
Production	G-BFKX[4]	216	April 79	

1 Later F-BTSC. 2 Later F-BTSD. 3 Later G-BOAG. 4 Later G-BOAF.

Individual aircraft data*

Aircraft Registration	Aircraft No.	Representative month – September 1985				Delivery – September 1985		
		Hours flown	Braked landings	Supersonic cycles	Total landings	Hours flown	Total landings	Supersonic cycles
G-BOAA	206	95	32	24	32	9640	3483	2722
G-BOAB	208	98	43	27	43	9413	3446	2659
G-BOAC	204	32	16	4	16	8706	3258	2479
G-BOAD	210	88	27	27	27	9498	3146	2679
G-BOAE	212	122	44	43	44	9525	3649	2683
G-BOAF	216	131	54	44	54	4633	1494	1397
G-BOAG	214	121	42	34	42	1932	632	577
Totals		687	258	204	258	53347	19108	15196

Fleet Operational Data – 1985 (September)**

Concorde	Jan	Feb	Mar	Apr	May	Jun	Jul	Aug	Sept	Oct	Nov	Dec
Aircraft in service	6	6	6	6	7	7	7	7	7			
Flying hours	429	497	575	561	595	609	602	478	687			
Daily utilisation	2.31	2.96	3.09	3.12	2.74	2.90	2.77	2.20	3.27			
Scheduled departures	150	166	195	186	204	207	211	180	258			
Supersonic cycles	129	153	188	178	199	201	201	159	204			
Total landings	150	276	202	201	204	207	211	185	258			
Braked landings	150	187	196	188	204	207	211	180	258			
Average flight time	2.86	1.80	2.85	2.79	2.92	2.94	2.85	2.58	2.66			

British Airways Concorde crews during the first ten years*

Captains

R. P. W. Allen
R. J. L. Boas
J. A. D. Bradshaw
D. A. Brister
N. A. Britton
A. L. Budd
J. W. Burton
B. J. Calvert
J. L. Chorley
J. D. Cook
R. V. Dixon
P. R. W. Duffey
J. D. Eames
D. H. Ellis
J. W. Hirst
J. C. Hutchinson
K. D. Leney
H. J. Linfield
A. J. Massie
C. B. McMahon
H. C. McMullen
I. C. McNeilly
A. R. Meadows
C. J. C. Morley
C. C. Morris
K. Myers
D. J. M. Rendall
E. Reynolds
M. A. Riley
D. G. Ross
R. S. Smith
B. G. T. Titchener
N. V. Todd
B. O. Walpole

B. Irven
W. D. Lowe
D. G. Mitchell
C. E. Norris
B. R. Oliver
C. J. D. Orlebar
J. H. Phillingham
W. J. Piper
J. M. Reynolds
C. A. Robey
D. C. Rowland
W. I. Smith
R. J. Taylor
J. R. White
D. Whitton
K. Williams
M. R. Withey
M. R. Young

First Officers

R. P. Babbé
M. Bannister
M. E. Boyle
R. J. S. Burchell
M. W. Burke
A. D. Cobley
C. D. Green
A. I. Heald
B. R. Holland
P. W. Horton

Engineer Officers

S. L. Bolton
G. S. Bowden
R. C. Bricknell
A. A. Brown
W. J. Brown
M. Cooper
T. B. Dewis
W. Dobbs
P. E. Egginton
I. R. Fellowes-Freeman
S. G. Floyd
J. Goatham
W. G. Hornby
W. D. Johnston
W. A. Johnstone
I. V. Kirby
J. E. Lidiard
P. A. Ling
D. A. Macdonald
P. J. Newman
P. J. Phillips
J. A. Rodger
T. J. Quarrey
I. F. Smith
J. Stanbridge
G. Tullier
R. N. Webb
A. F. Winstanley

*This shows the analysis for September 1985 and the position since the aircraft were new. The 'rig' at Farnborough achieved 20,000 'equivalent' supersonic cycles. Before the total of supersonic flight cycles reaches one third of this total a review will take place, however there is no finite limit to the life of the airframe. There were 28 crews in 1980, in January 1986 there were 20.

**This shows the data up to September for the year 1985. Note that during February, March and April, when conversion training was in progress, the number of landings exceeded the number of 'braked landings'. During training, rather than stopping after a landing, thrust is reapplied, the aircraft taking-off once the appropriate speed has been attained. In May 1985 G-BOAG re-entered service.

Concorde chronology

1956
November 5: Supersonic Transport Aircraft Committee (STAC) established.

1959
March 9: STAC recommends design studies of two supersonic airliners (Mach 1.2 and Mach 2).

1959–61
French and British SST feasibility and design studies initiated.

1961
First Anglo-French discussions on possible SST collaboration. *June–July:* First BAC/Sud discussions in Paris and Weybridge.

1962
October: Anglo-French Mach 2.2 transport specification published. *November 29:* Anglo-French agreement for joint design development and manufacture of a supersonic airliner.

1963
Preliminary design presented to airlines. *January 13:* President de Gaulle uses name 'Concorde'. *June 3:* Concorde sales option signed by Pan American Airlines. *June:* BOAC and Air France sign Concorde sales options. *June 5:* US supersonic transport programme announced.

1964
Projected medium-range version abandoned; design of long-range version enlarged. *May:* Enlarged Concorde design announced. *July:* Olympus 593D first run, Bristol.

1965
April: Metal cut for Concorde prototypes. *May:* Pre-production Concorde design announced.

1966 Manufacturer – and airline engineering liaison established. *April:* Final assembly of prototype 001 begins, Toulouse. *June:* Concorde flight simulator commissioned. *August:* Assembly of prototype 002 begins at Filton. *September:* First flight of Avro Vulcan testbed with Olympus 593 engine. *October:* Olympus 593 achieves 35,190 lb thrust on test at Bristol. *December:* Fuselage section delivered to RAE, Farnborough for fatigue testing.

1967
Design for pre-production aircraft revised to reduce drag; rear fuselage extended; new nose/visor. *February:* Concorde interior mock-up presented to airlines at Filton. *April:* Complete Olympus 593 engine first test-run in high altitude chamber, Saclay. *December 11:* 001 rolled out at Toulouse. British partner adopted 'Concorde' spelling.

1968
February: UK Government announces £125m loan for Concorde production. *August:* 001 taxi trials, Toulouse. *September:* rolled out at Toulouse. British aircraft design redefined. *December:* Olympus 593 ground-testing reaches 5,000 hours. *December 31:* First flight of Tupolev Tu-144 prototype.

1969
March 2: First flight of 001, Toulouse. *March:* Government authority given for construction of nine airframes (two ground test airframes, two prototypes, two pre-production aircraft and three production aircraft). *April 9:* First flight of 002, Filton (to Fairford). *June:* First public appearance of both prototypes, Paris air show. *October 1:* 001 achieves Mach 1. *November 8:* Airline pilots fly 001. *December:* Authority given for construction of three more production aircraft.

1970
March 25: 002 achieves Mach 1. *September 1:* 002 appears at SBAC show, Farnborough; lands at Heathrow. *November 4:* 001 achieves Mach 2. *November 12:* 002 achieves Mach 2.

1971
January: 100th supersonic flight. *March 24:* Congress stops US supersonic transport programme. *April:* Authority given for four more production aircraft. *May 25:* 001 appears at Paris air show; flies to Dakar. *June:* Total Concorde flight test time reaches 500 hours. *August:* 100th Mach 2 flight. *September 20:* First pre-production Concorde, 01 rolled out at Filton. *December 17:* First flight of 01, Filton.

1972
February 12: 01 exceeds Mach 1. *April 13:* Production aircraft 11–16 authorised. *April 22–23:* 002 appears at Hanover air show. *May 25:* BOAC announces intention to order five Concordes. *June:* 002 sales demonstration tour of Middle East and Australia. *July 24:* China signs preliminary purchase agreement for two Concordes. *July 28:* BOAC orders five Concordes, Air France orders four. *August 28:* China signs preliminary purchase agreement for a third Concorde. *September 28:* Concorde 02 rolled out at Toulouse. *October 5:* Iran Air signs preliminary purchase agreement for two Concordes plus option on a third.

1973
January 10: First flight of 02, Toulouse. *January 22–February 24:* 002 completes 'hot and high' trials at Johannesburg. *January 31:* Pam American and TWA decide not to take up their Concorde options. *June 3:* Production Tupolev Tu 144 crashes during Paris Air Show. *June 30:* 001 flight to Fort Lamy (Chad) gives 80-minute scientific observation of solar eclipse. *September 18:* 02 leaves Paris for first US visit for opening of Dallas/Fort Worth Airport. *September 26:* Breaks Washington–Paris record (3 hr 33 min) on return flight. *October 19:* 001 retired to French Air Museum at Le Bourget. *December 6:* First flight of 201, first production Concorde.

1974
February 7–19: 02 completes low-temperature trials at Fairbanks, Alaska. *February 13:* First flight of 202, second production Concorde (G-BBDG). *June 25:* Concorde static test specimen at CEAT tested to destruction. *July 19:* Initial production programme of 16 aircraft agreed. *August:* Middle East demonstration flights by 202. *September 12:* Flight testing total reaches 3,000 hours. *October 20–28:* American Pacific coast demonstration tour. *October 21:* Supersonic flight total reaches 1,000 hours.

1975
January 31: First flight of 203. *February 11:* Completion of passenger emergency evacuation certification trials. *February:* Tropical icing trials. *February 27:* First flight of 204. *February:* Certification trials at Madrid. *May 28:* Special-category C of A for 203 awarded; registration changed to F-BTSC; start of 'endurance' flying by this aircraft (completed August 2nd). *May:* Static display and flying programme at Paris air show. *June 30:* CAA special-category C of A for 204 awarded. *October 9:* Concorde receives French C of A. *October 14:* British Airways and Air France open reservations for Concorde scheduled services. *October 25:* First flight by 205. *November 5:* First flight by 206. *November 13:* Final Environmental Impact Statement published by FAA. *December 5:* Concorde receives British C of A. *December 19:* Air France receives its first Concorde (205).

1976
January 5: Concorde public hearing held by US Secretary of Transportation. *January 6:* Air France receives 203. *January 15:* British Airways receives its first Concorde (206). *January 21:* Airline service begins; London–Bahrain (British Airways, 206) and Paris–Rio via Dakar (Air France, 205). *February 4:* Concorde services to New York and Washington for 16-months trial period approved by US Secretary of Transportation. *February 13:* British Airways receives its second Concorde (204). *March 4:* 002 retired to Science Museum (based at RN Air Station, Yeovilton). *March 6:* First flight of 207. *April 8:* Air France receives 207. *April 9:* Air France service extended to Caracas via Santa Maria, Azores. *May 18:* First flight of 208. *May 20:* 02 retired to Orly Airport, Paris. *May 24:* Transatlantic services begin, from Paris and London to Washington. *July 9:* First flight of 209. *August 3:* Air France receives 209. *August 25:* First flight of 210. *September 30:* British Airways receives its third Concorde (208). *November 30:* Fairford flight test base closed. *December 6:* British Airways receives 210. *December 8:* Concorde 203 returned by Air France to Aérospatiale.

1977
February 10: First flight of 211. *March 17:* First flight of 212. *March 26:* Air France receives 211. *July 20:* British Airways receives 212. *August 20:* 01 retired to Duxford, under care of Imperial War Museum. *October 19:* Proving flights to New York begin. *October 26:* Singapore Airlines/BA agreement on London–Singapore flights via Bahrain announced. *November 2:* H.M. The Queen and Prince Philip return from Barbados on Concorde. *November 22:* Services to New York begin, from Paris and London. *December 9:* Service from London to Singapore via Bahrain begins.

1978
Prolonged talks on Malaysian Concorde ban. *April 21:* First flight of 214. *June 26:* First flight of 213. *August 10:* BA carries its 100,000th Concorde passenger. *September 18:* Air France receives 213. *September 20:* Air France opens service Paris to Mexico City via Washington. *December 26:* First flight of 215.

1979
January 9: US type certificate awarded. *January 12:* Braniff subsonic service between Washington and Dallas/Fort Worth inaugurated. *January 24:* BA/Singapore Airlines extension Bahrain–Singapore resumed. *February 22:* British Government announces BA to write off Concorde purchase cost; Government to receive 80 per cent of operating surpluses. *April 20:* First flight of last production Concorde (216), Filton. *September 21:* British and French Governments announce unsold aircraft and support engines to be placed with British Airways and Air France. *December 16:* BA Concorde flies London–New York in 2 hr 59 min 36 sec.

1980
February 6: British Airways receives 214. *June 1:* Braniff ceases Dallas/Fort Worth service. *June 13:* British Airways receives 216. *October 23:* Air France receives 215. *November 1:* Singapore service discontinued.

1981
January 21: Five years in airline service: 50,000 hours, 15,800 flights, 700,000 passengers. *January–February:* Evidence on Concorde presented to Commons Industry and Trade Committee. *April 14:* Report on Concorde published by Commons Industry and Trade Committee expresses dissatisfaction with cost figures and urges efforts to ensure costs are shared equally with France. Government reply in July describes committee's criticisms of forecasts as 'unwarranted'. *September 11:* Anglo-French 'summit' meeting: British and French Governments commission joint studies on future of Concorde. *October 29:* British and French ministers meet in London to discuss Concorde. Three options proposed: (1) cancellation; (2) a phased rundown; (3) indefinite continuation. *December 2:* British Government review of relative costs presented to Parliament by Department of Industry. *December 9:* Department of Industry ministers and officials give evidence to Commons Industry and Trade Committee.

Concorde chronology

1982

March 31: Air France services to Caracas and Rio discontinued. *February:* British Industry and Trade Committee reaffirm dissatisfaction with cost aspects. *May 1:* Formation of Concorde Division within British Airways, responsible for profitability of Concorde operations. *May 6:* British and French ministers meet in Paris to discuss Concorde (cost reductions, officials' report, cost-sharing). *August:* Ian Sproat (Government Minister responsible) writes to Chairman of BA Sir John King stating that the Government will cease to fund Concorde's British manufacturers (Rolls-Royce and British Aerospace). *October:* Sir John King replies to the Sproat letter saying that BA will examine the possibility of Concorde funding the support costs out of revenue. *November:* Group set up within BA to examine support costs.

1983

January 1: Fastest transatlantic crossing west to east: New York to London in 2 hours 56 minutes. *April 13:* BBC television documentary about Concorde in the QED series broadcast.

1984

March 27: Concorde inaugural to Miami through Washington. Henceforward a thrice weekly service to Miami. *March 31:* After eighteen months of negotiations British Government involvement in the Concorde project becomes minimal with BA becoming responsible for funding Concorde's British manufacturers. *September 11:* Distance record Washington–Nice by G-BOAB 3,965 nm (4,255 statue miles). *November 16:* Concorde (G-BOAB) inaugural charter to Seattle from London via New York.

1985

February 13: First commercial service London–Sydney by Concorde under charter establishing a record time of 17 hours and 3 minutes. *March 28:* Concorde under a commercial charter establishes the record between London and Cape Town of 8 hours and 8 minutes. *April 25:* New livery unveiled by Concorde G-BOAG (214) returning into service. This aircraft had been out of service for a long period with much of its equipment having been removed for use in the other Concordes. *May 11:* Concorde special charter inaugural to Pittsburg. *Dec 19:* Highest recorded ground speed, to date, achieved by Concorde G-BOAC in commercial service, 1,292 kt (1,488 mph).

Throughout 1985 Concorde inaugurates several routes within Europe for publicity reasons and to destinations within the Americas in conjunction with the Cunard Shipping Line.

1986

January 21: Concorde celebrates 10 years of commercial operations. *July 11:* Prime Minister Margaret Thatcher makes her first supersonic flight on Concorde from London to Vancouver to visit EXPO 86. She is presented with a copy of *The Concorde Story*. *November 8–23:* Concorde's first round-the-world charter, special edition of *The Concorde Story* commissioned by John Player to mark the event.

British Airways (BA) Concorde destinations as of November 1986 from London Airport (Heathrow)

Current Scheduled Services
New York *twice daily*
Miami (via Washington)*
Washington*
   thrice weekly

Past Scheduled Services
Bahrain
Singapore

Diversions
Atlantic City
Bangor
Boston
Gander
Halifax
Lajes
Montreal
Newark
Shannon
Windsor Locks

Charter destinations

The Americas
Antigua
Aruba
Atlanta
Baltimore
Barbados
Bermuda
Calgary
Cleveland
Colorado Springs
Columbus
Dayton
Detroit
Fort Lauderdale
Grand Cayman
Harrisburg
Houston
Indianapolis
Lima
Miami
Nassau
New Orleans
New York
Oklahoma City
Omaha
Ontario
Orlando

Oshkosh
Philadelphia
Pittsburgh
Port-of-Spain
Puerto Rico
Raleigh
Rio de Janeiro
Rochester
Rockford
St Lucia
Santa Maria
Seattle
Syracuse
Tampa
Toronto
Trinidad
Vancouver
Waco
Washington

Europe and Mid-East
Amsterdam
Ancona
Bahrain
Barcelona
Basle
Berlin
Billund
Bordeaux
Brussels
Budapest
Cairo
Cologne
Copenhagen
Dhahran
Graz
Helsinki
Istanbul
Keflavik
Kuwait
Larnaca
Leipzig
Linz
Lisbon
Madrid
Malaga
Marrakesh
Milan
Moscow
Munich
Nice

Oslo
Palma
Paris
Prague
Riyadh
Rome
Rovaniemi
Salzburg
Stockholm
Tel Aviv
Tours
Turin
Venice
Vienna

Far East
Bangkok
Colombo
Hong Kong
Singapore

Southern Hemisphere
Auckland
Cape Town
Djakarta
Perth
Sydney

United Kingdom
Belfast
Birmingham
Cardiff
East Midlands
Edinburgh
Fairford
Filton
Finningley
Gatwick
Glasgow
Leuchars
Liverpool
Manston
Mildenhall
Newcastle
Prestwick
Teeside
Yeovilton

Air France Concorde destinations from Charles de Gaulle Airport (Paris)

Current Scheduled Service
New York *once daily*

Past Scheduled Services
Rio de Janeiro (via Dakar)
Caracas (Santa Maria)
Washington
Mexico (via Washington)

Note: Air France also handles Concorde charters, but these destinations have not been listed.

Index

Bibliography

An Introduction to the Slender, Delta Transport, BAC/Aerospatiale, 1975

British Airways and Concorde Finances, Report of the Review Group, Department of Trade and Industry, February 1984.

David Beaty, *The Water Jump,* Secker & Warburg, 1976.

Charles Burnet, *Three Centuries to Concorde,* MEP, 1979.

Dr. P. H. Calder and P. C. Gupta, *Future SST Engines,* SAE, 1975.

Brian Calvert, *Flying Concorde,* Airlife, 1981.

Concorde, Second Report from the Industry and Trade Committee, Session 1980–81.

Flight International – various articles.

P. C. Gupta, Rolls-Royce Ltd., Aero Div., Bristol, *Advanced Olympus for Next Generation Supersonic Transport Aircraft,* SAE, 1981.

History of Aviation, New English Library, 1972.

Sir Stanley Hooker, *Not Much of an Engineer,* Airlife, 1984.

Jane's All the World's Aircraft – various editions.

Geoffrey Knight, *Concorde, The Inside Story,* Weidenfeld & Nicolson, 1976.

Sir Frank Whittle, *Jet, the Story of a Pioneer,* (Frederick Muller, 1953).

C. S. Leyman BAe, Bristol, *After Concorde What Next?,* (Presentation at A.I.A.A. annual meeting, Washington, 1985).

J. E. Morpurgo, *Barnes Wallis,* Longman, 1972.

Kenneth Owen, *Concorde, New Shape in the Sky,* Jane's, 1982.

Richard H. Peterson and Cornelius Driver, *Advanced Supersonic Transport Status,* (Presentation at A.I.A.A. annual meeting, Washington, April, 1985).

Arthur Reed, *Britain's Aircraft Industry, What went Right? What went Wrong?,* Dent, 1973.

Darrol Sinton, *The Anatomy of the Aeroplane,* Granada, 1966 (reprinted 1980).

Sir Basil Smallpeice, *Of Comets and Queens,* Airlife, 1981.

Illustration acknowledgements

Photographs and diagrams were kindly supplied by the following: *Aeroplane;* Aerospace Publishing Ltd; Peter A. Bisset; The Boeing Company; Braniff International; British Aerospace; British Tourist Authority; Avions Marcel Dassault; *Flight International;* Image in Industry; International Air Radio Ltd; Jack Leffler/Sky Eye Aerial Photographers; Adrian Meredith Photography; Metro Dade County; M. L. Nathan; National Aeronautics and Space Administration; Christopher Orlebar; Nigel Paige; Christine Quick Photography Ltd; RAF Museum; Rolls-Royce; Jeppesen Sanderson Inc; Tony Stone Associates; Syndication International; Michael Taylor; Michael Turner.

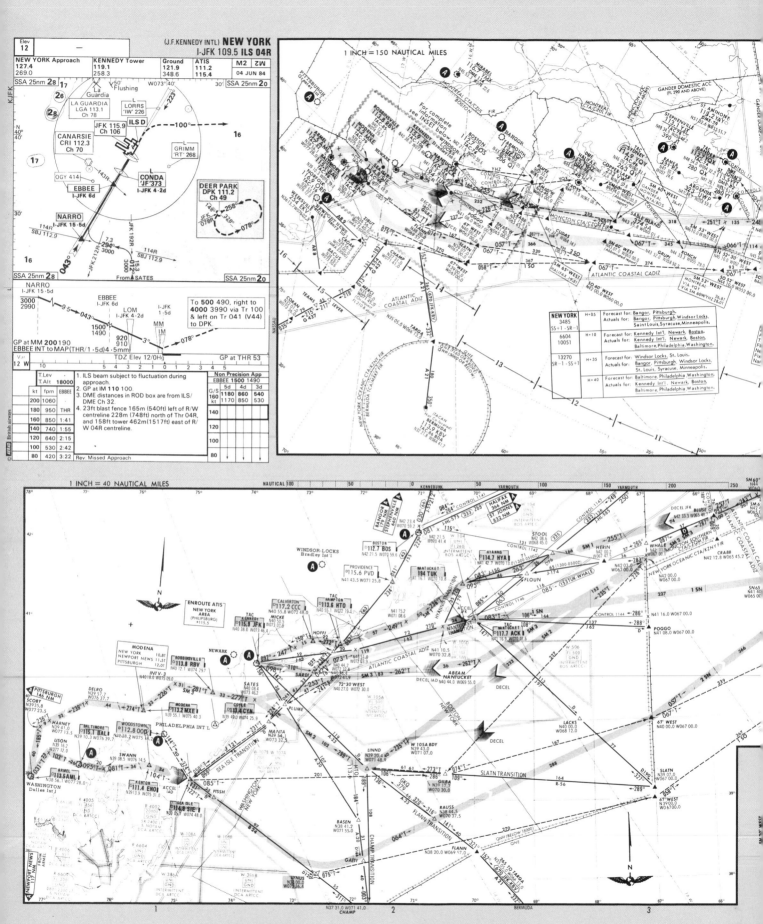